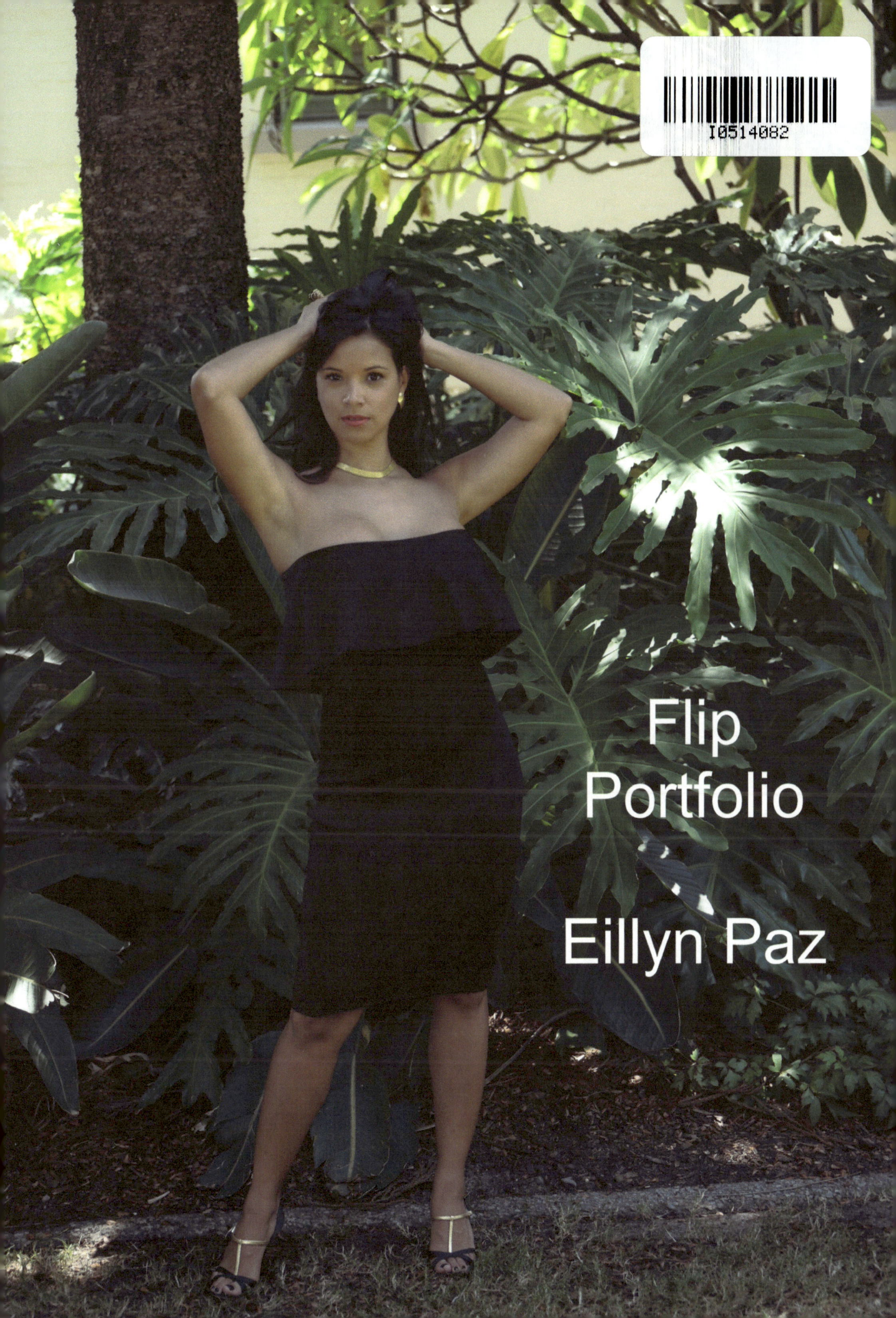

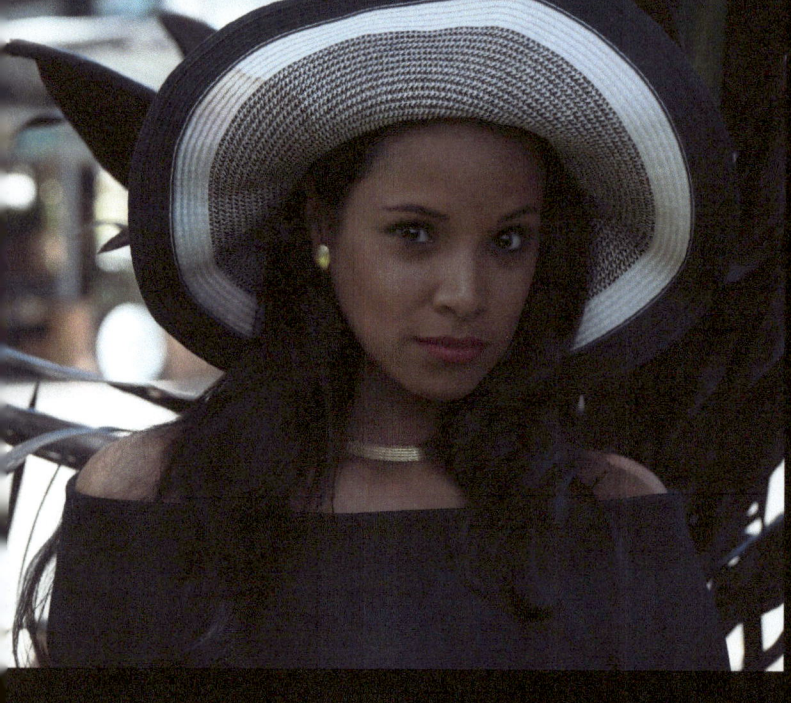
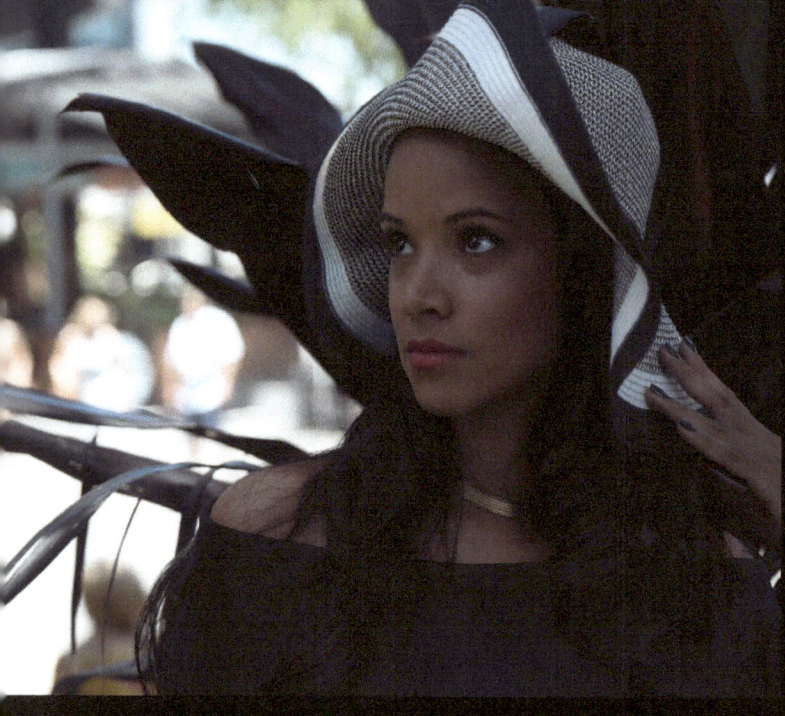
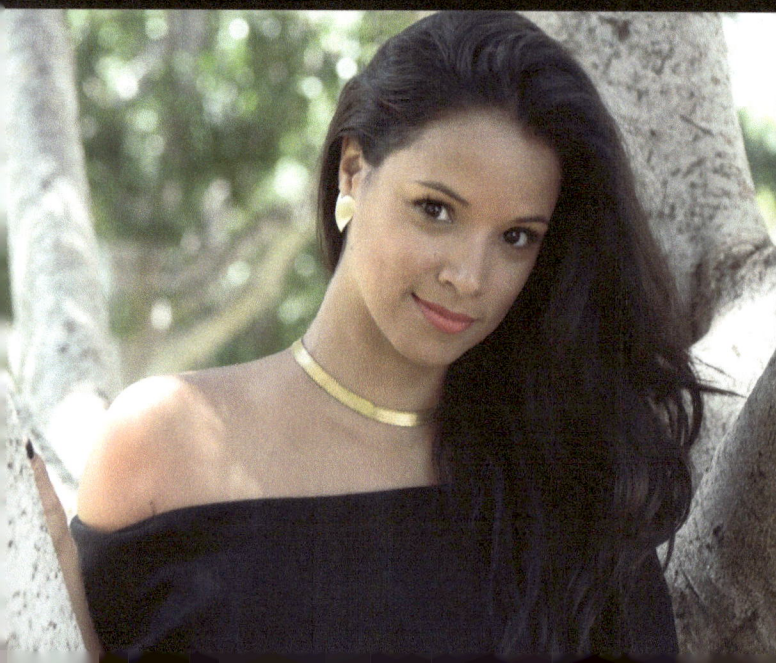

Flip Portfolio Eillyn Paz

ABN 55887680612

eillynpaz@gmail.com

Ethnicity
Mestizo/Latin
American-European

Height:
165 cms (5ft 6ins)

Weight:
63kgc (138lbs)

Bust:
94cms (37ins)

Waist:
78cms (31ins)

Hips:
98cms (38ins)

Hair:
Black

Eye Colour:
Black

Dress: 8-10

Shoes: 7

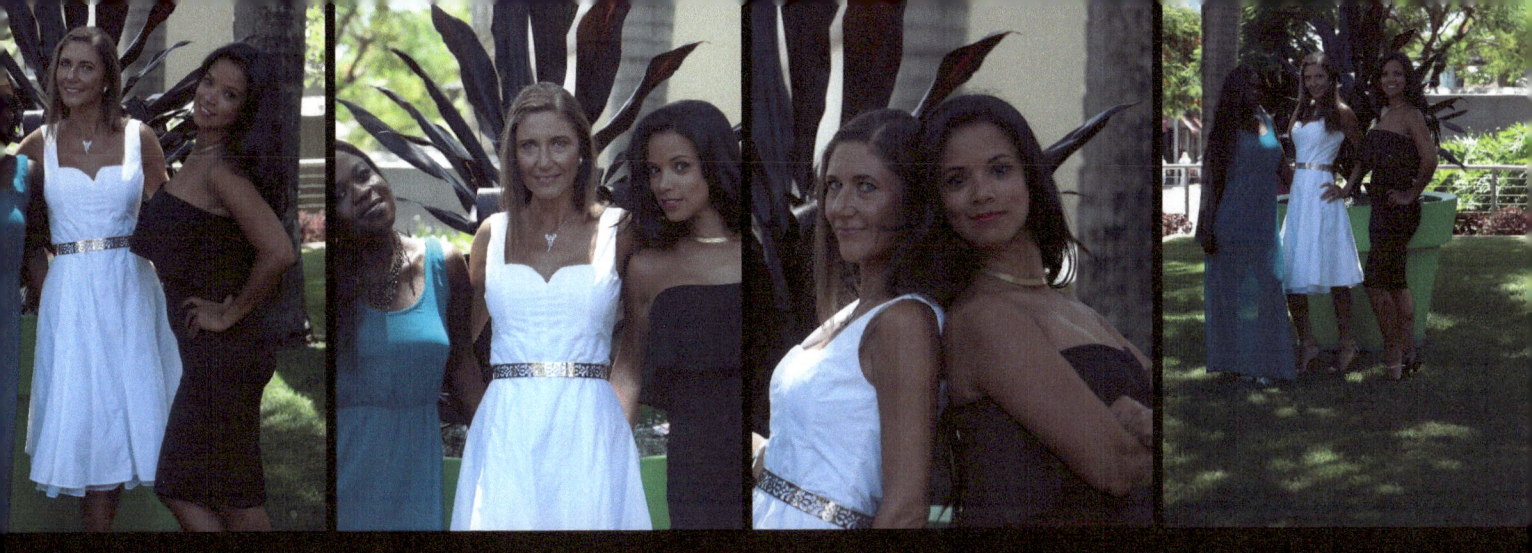

International Gisselle's Model Venezuela 2004

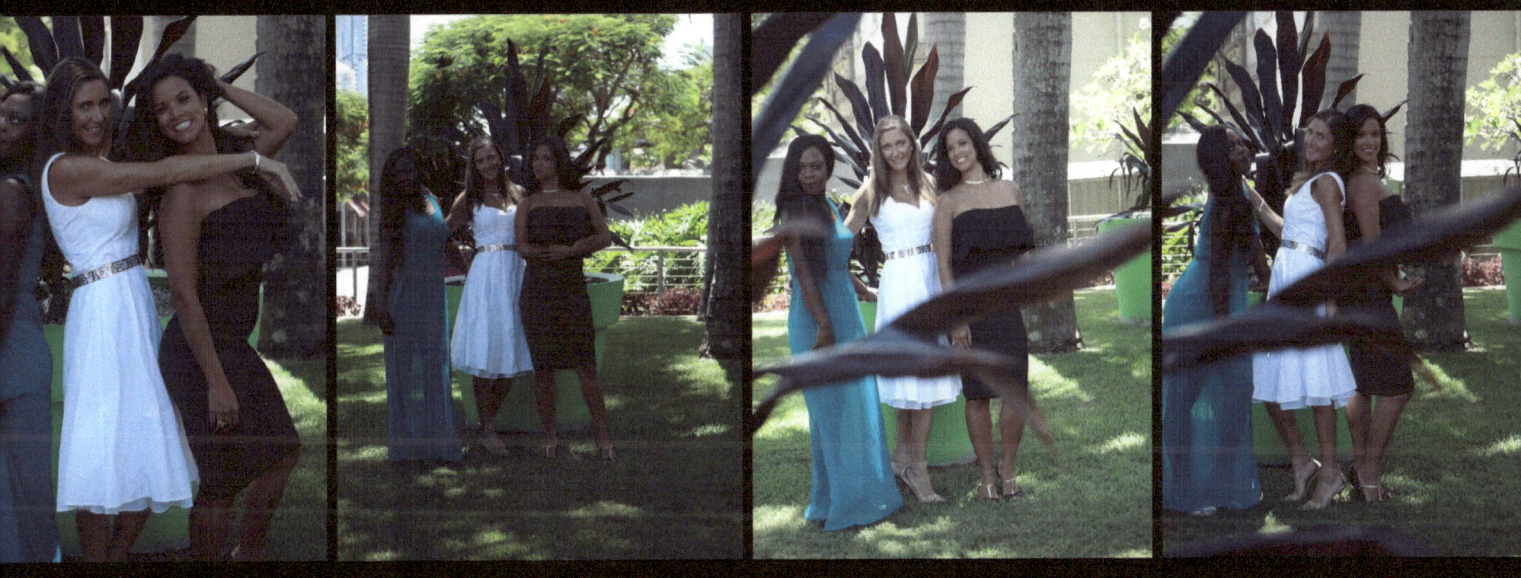

Miss Hawaiian Tropic Venezuela 2005

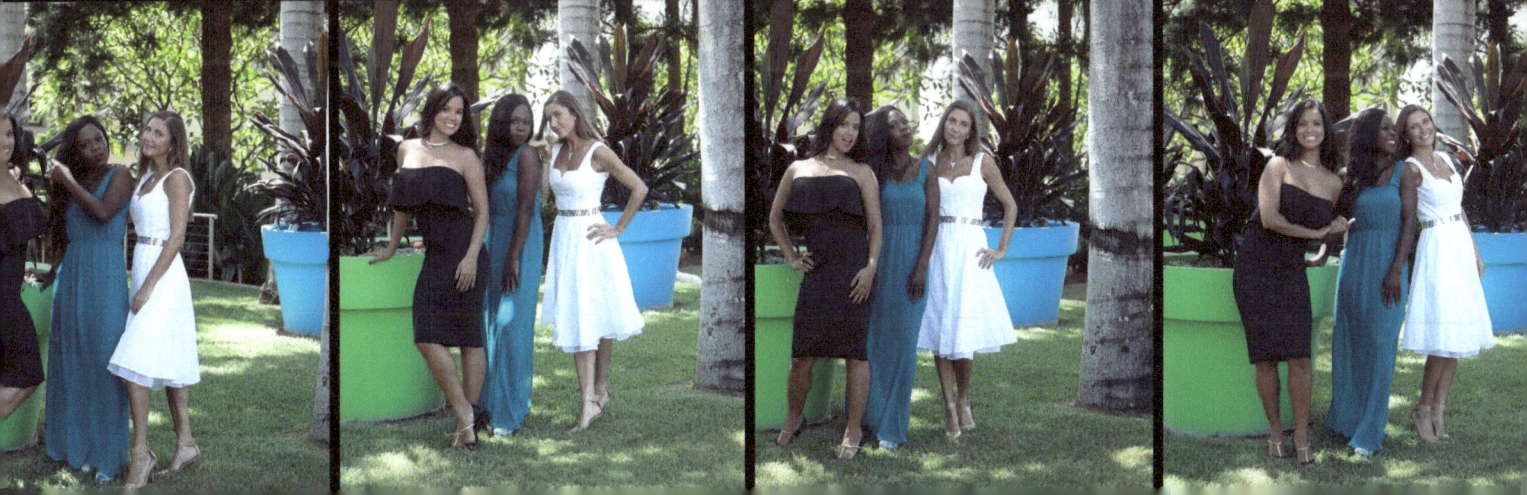

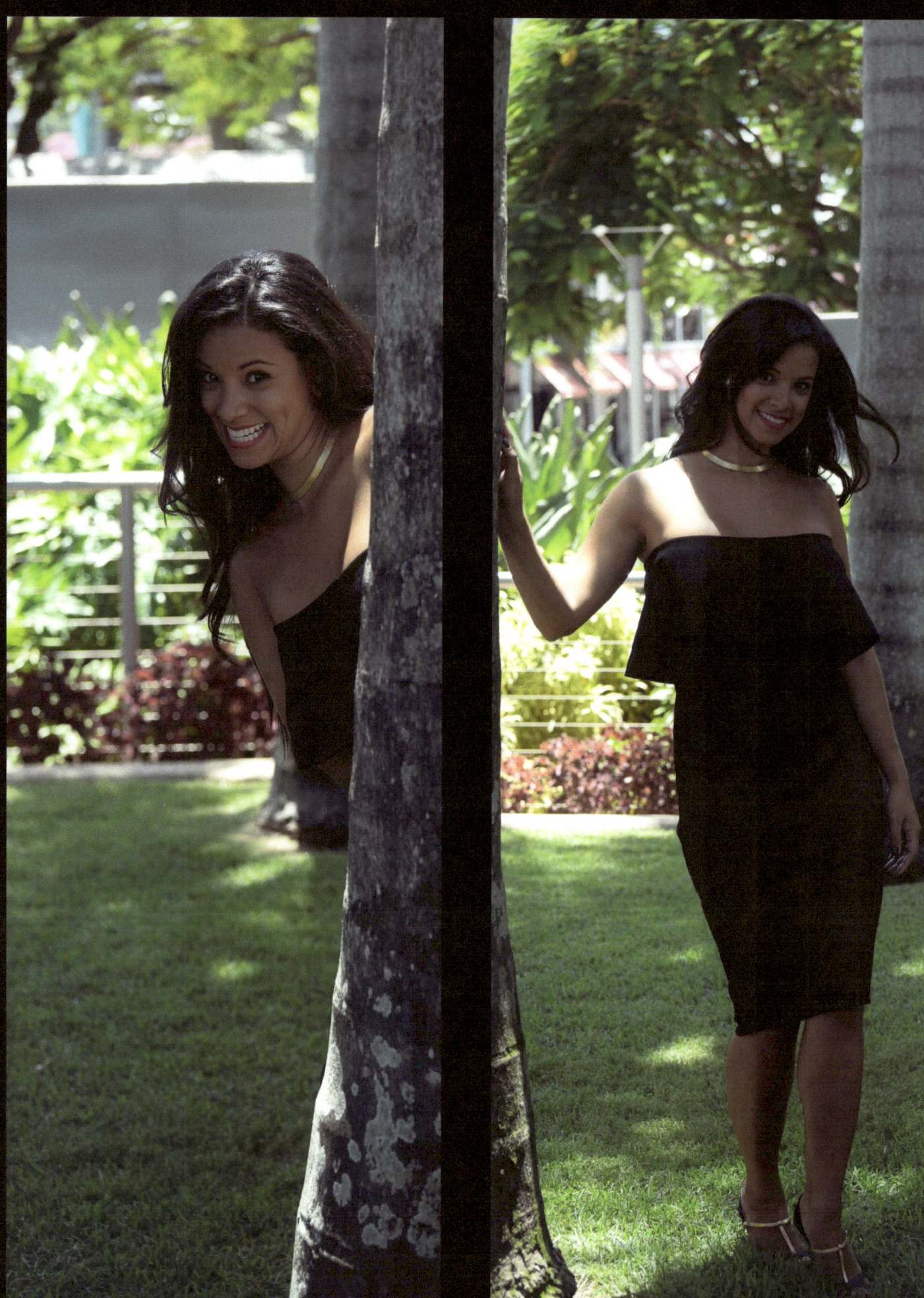

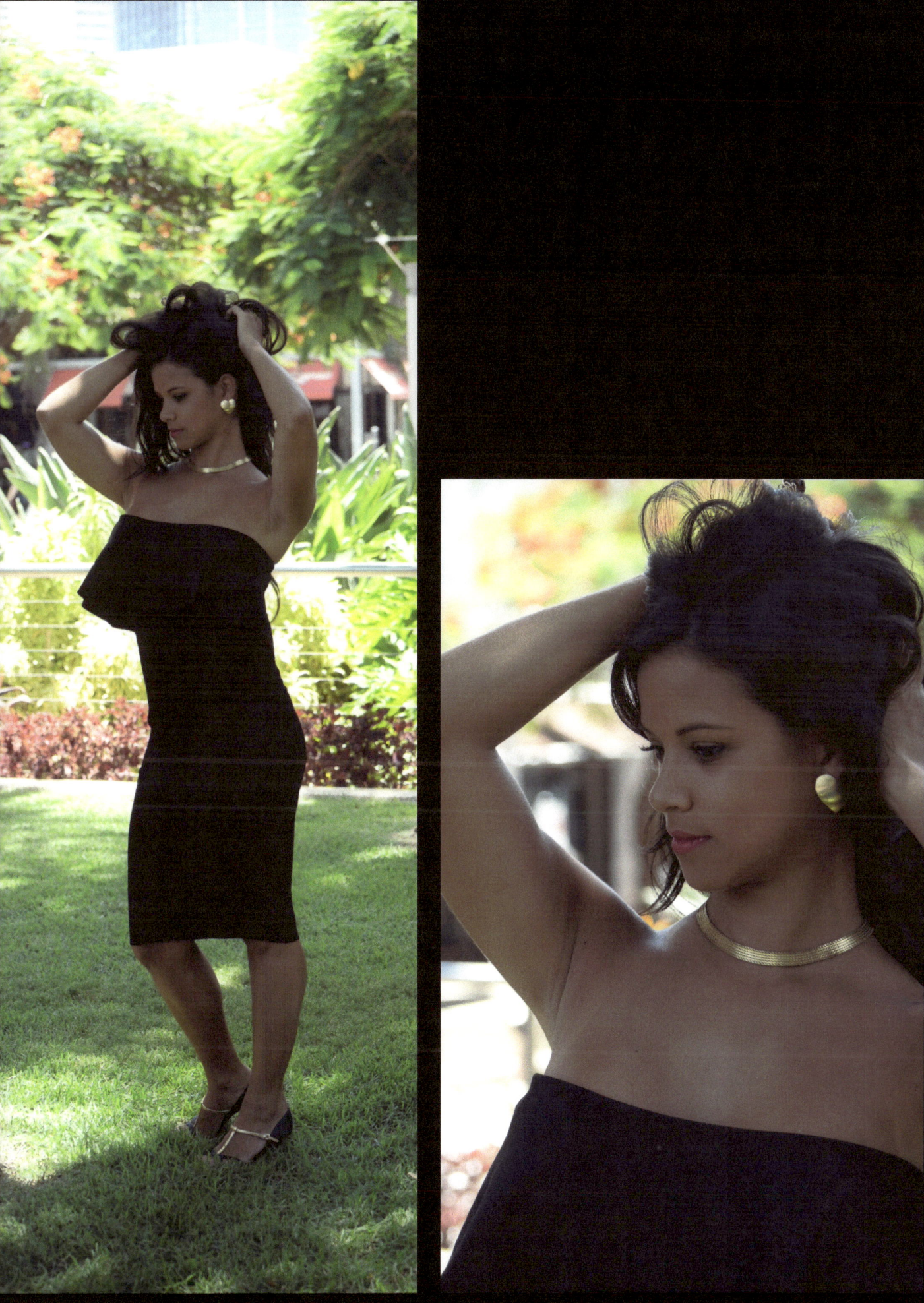

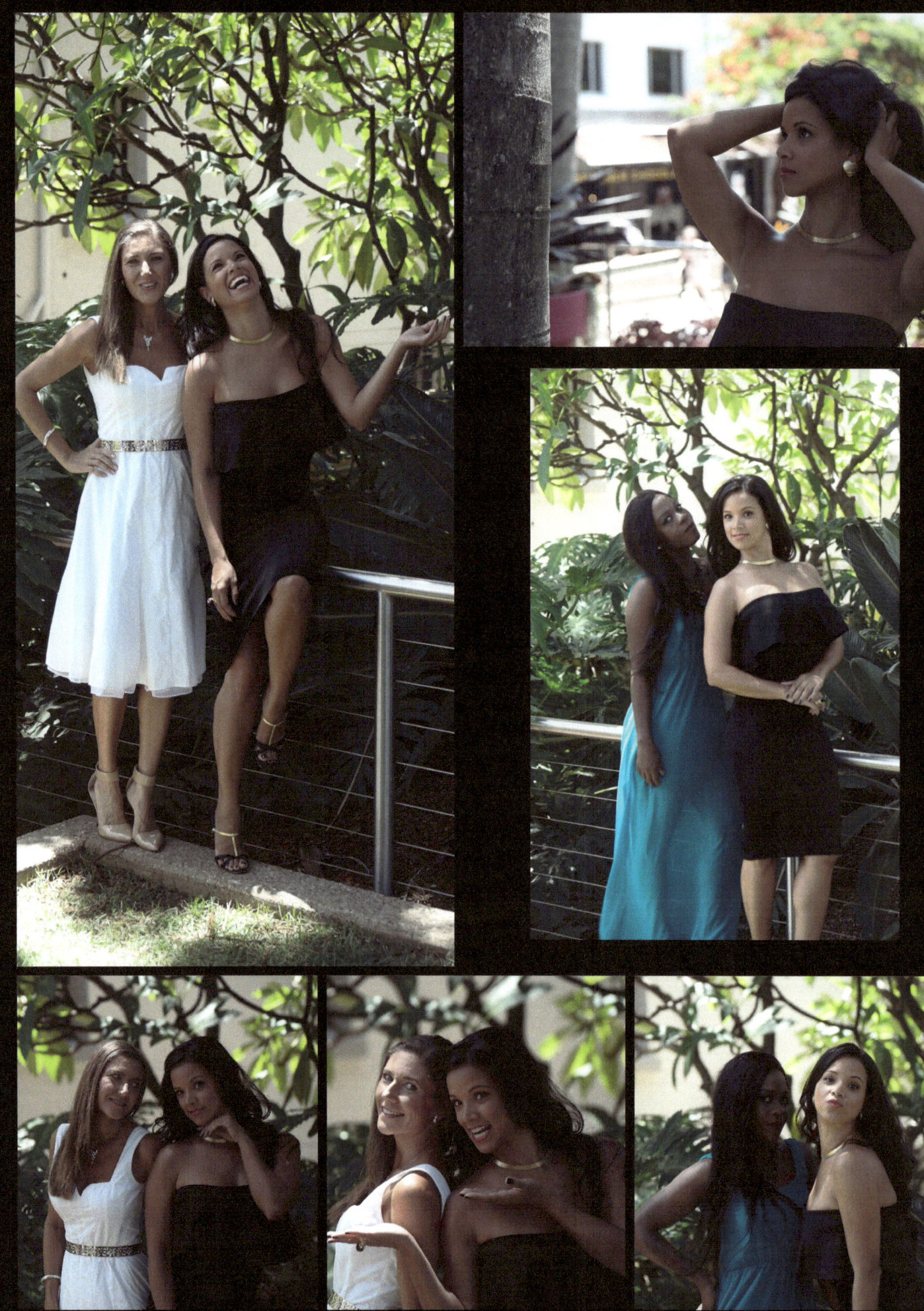

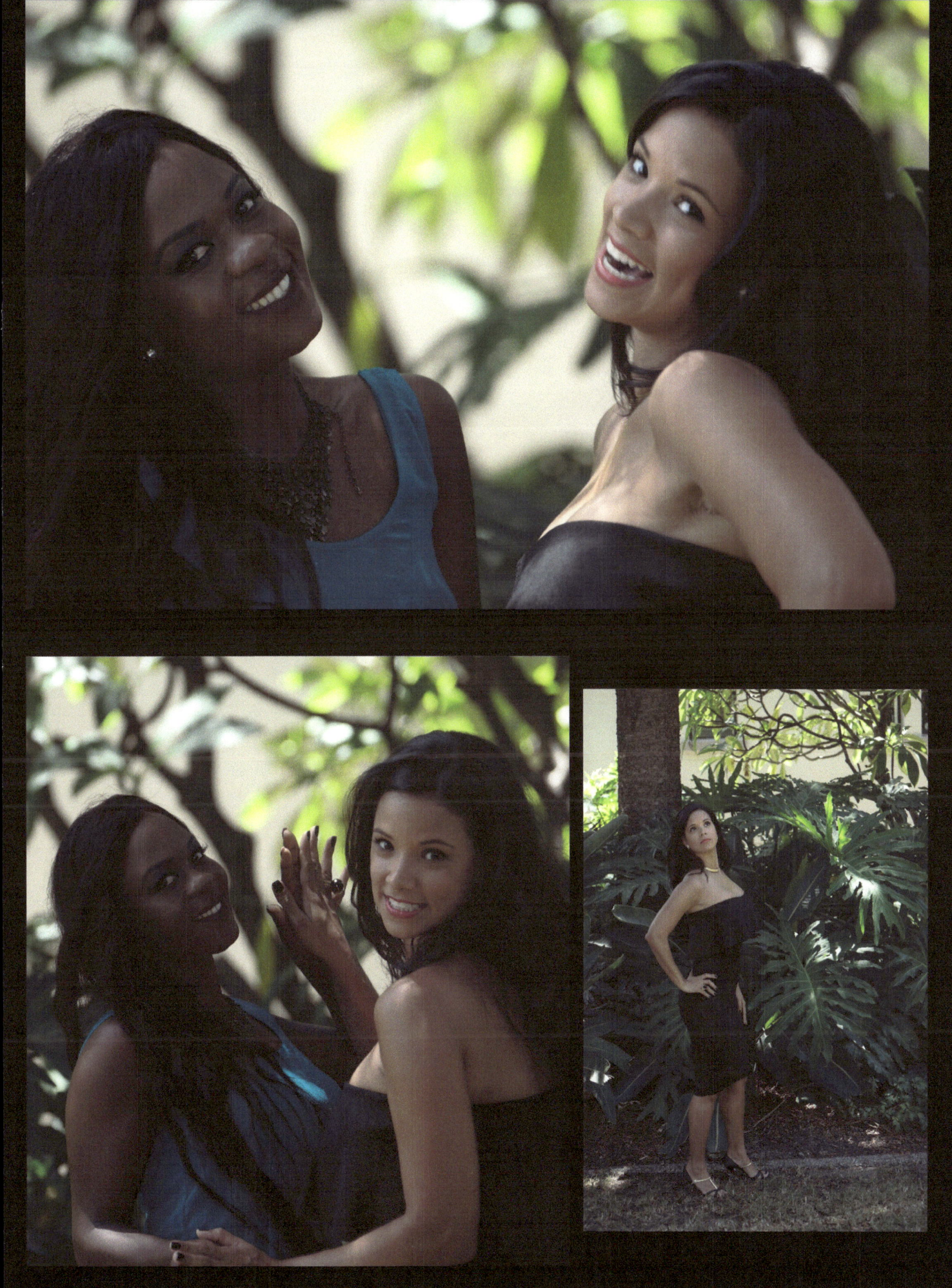

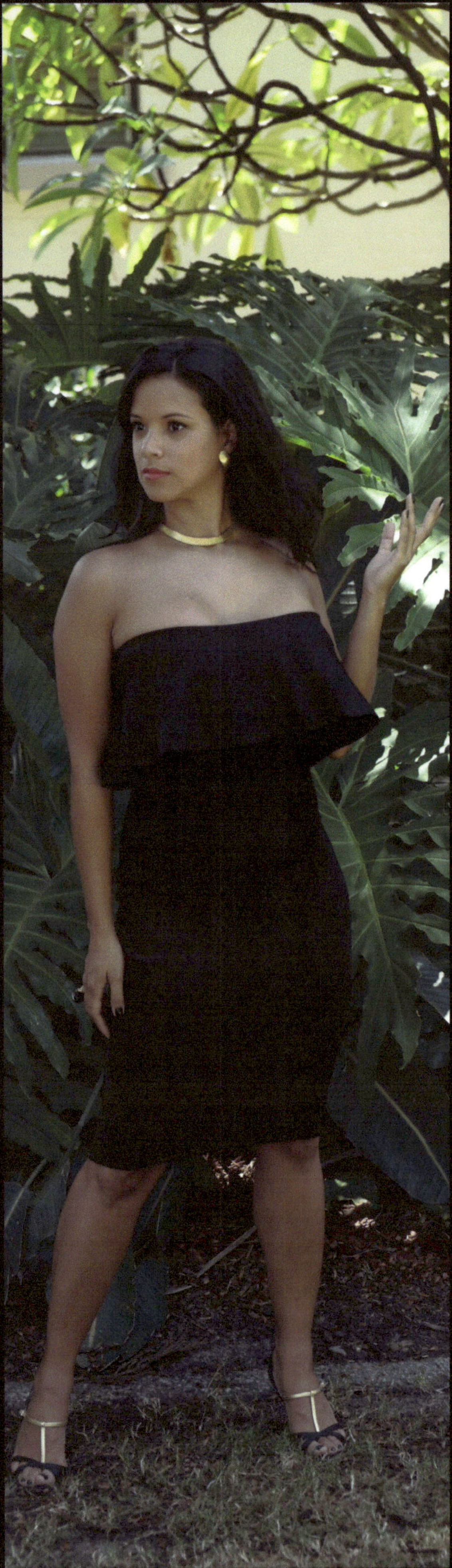

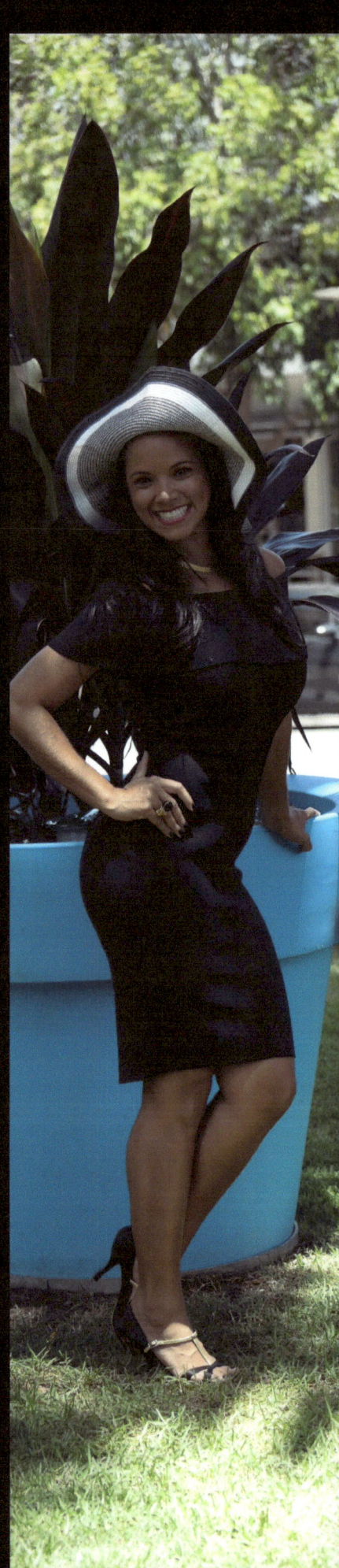
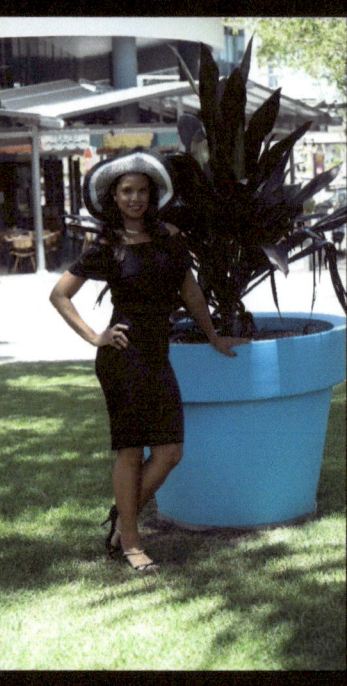
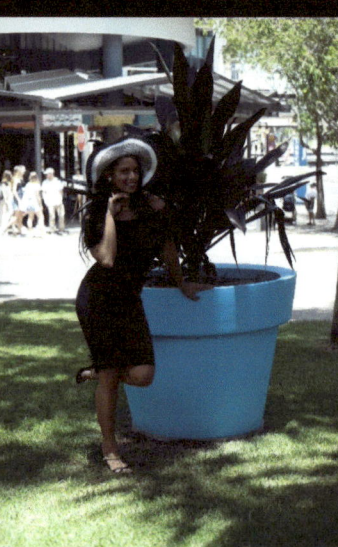
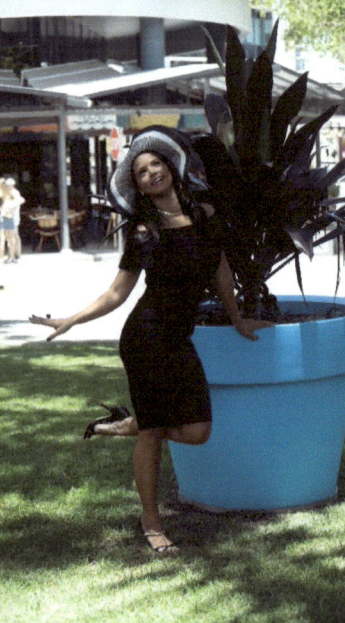

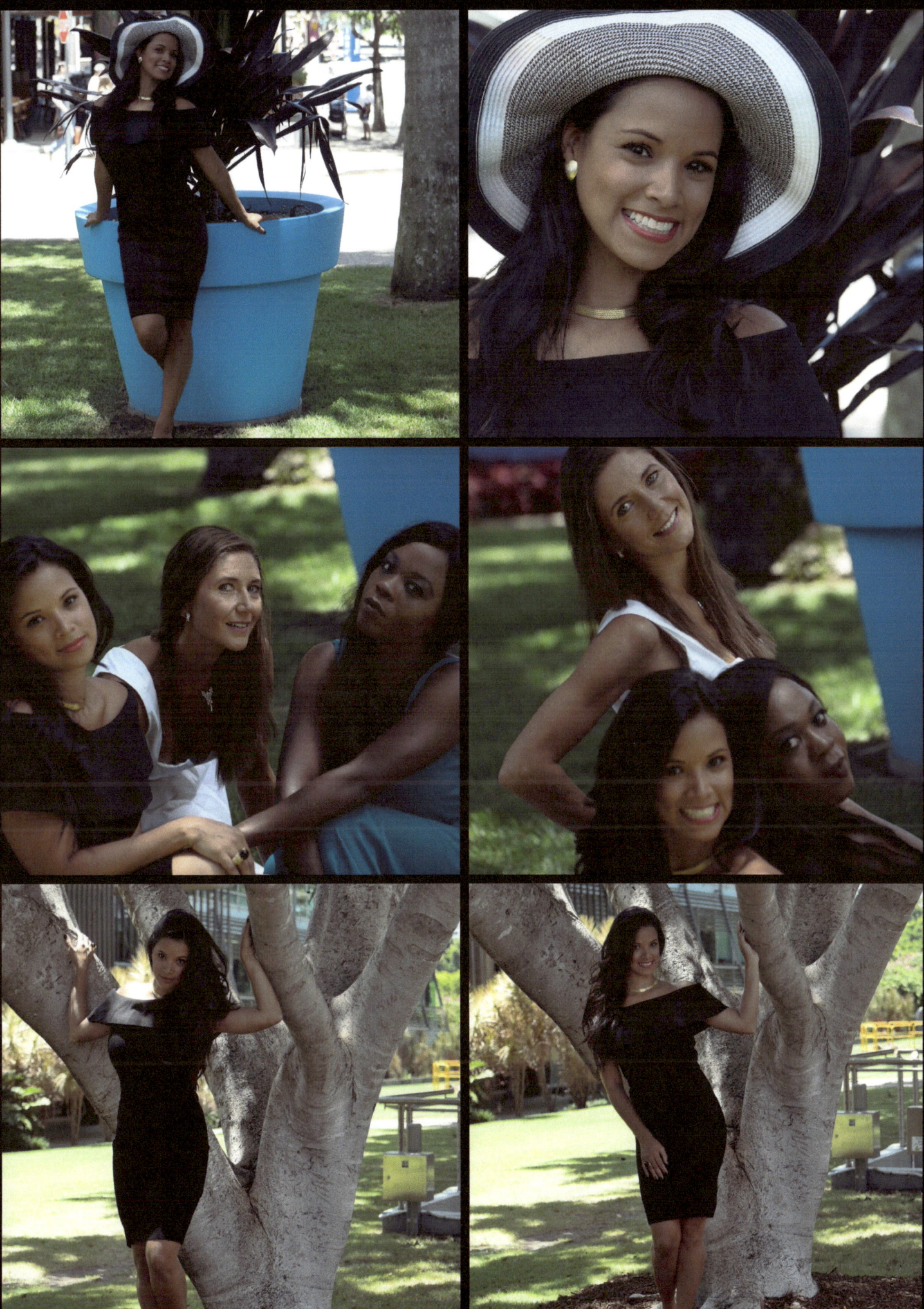

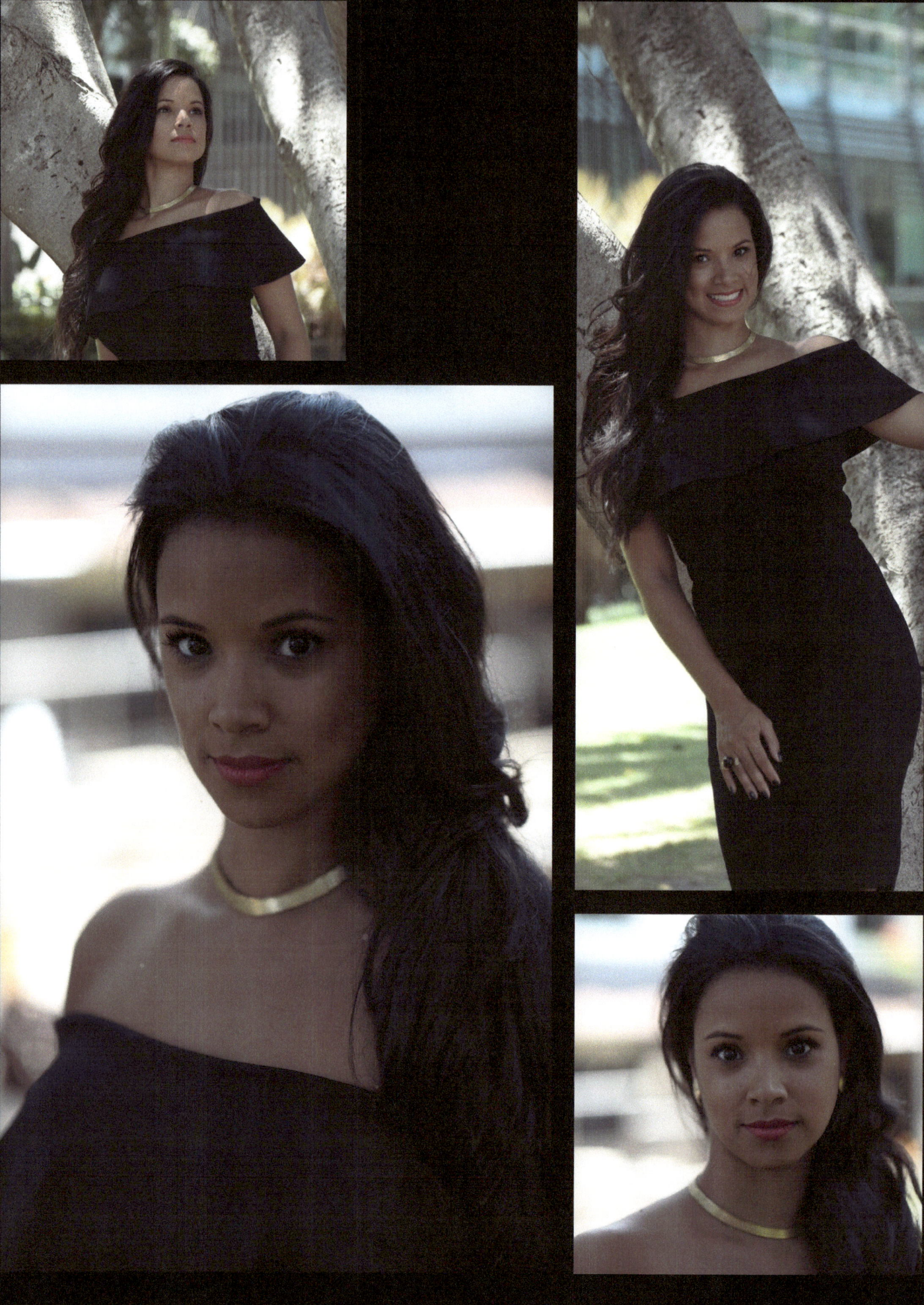

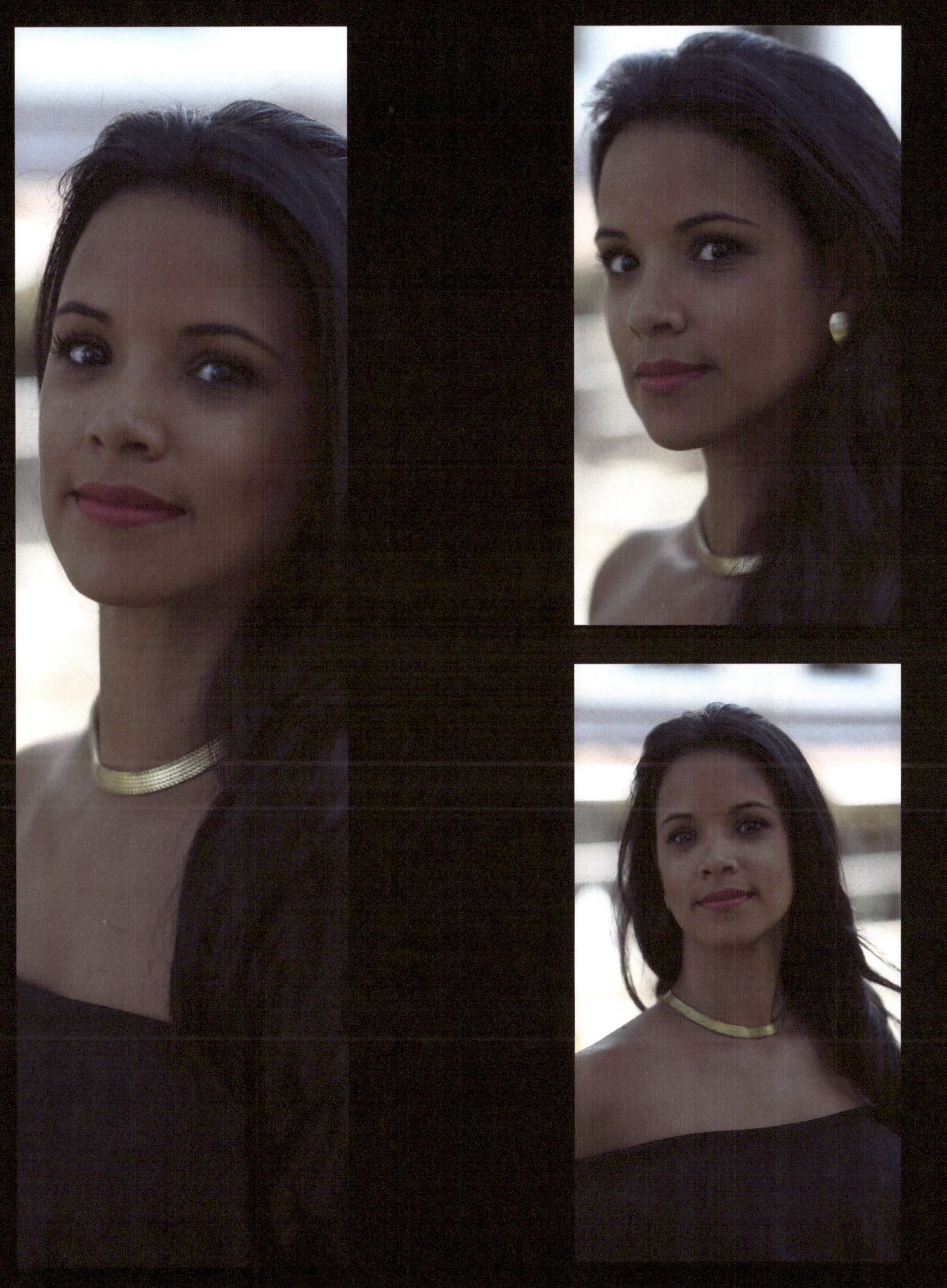

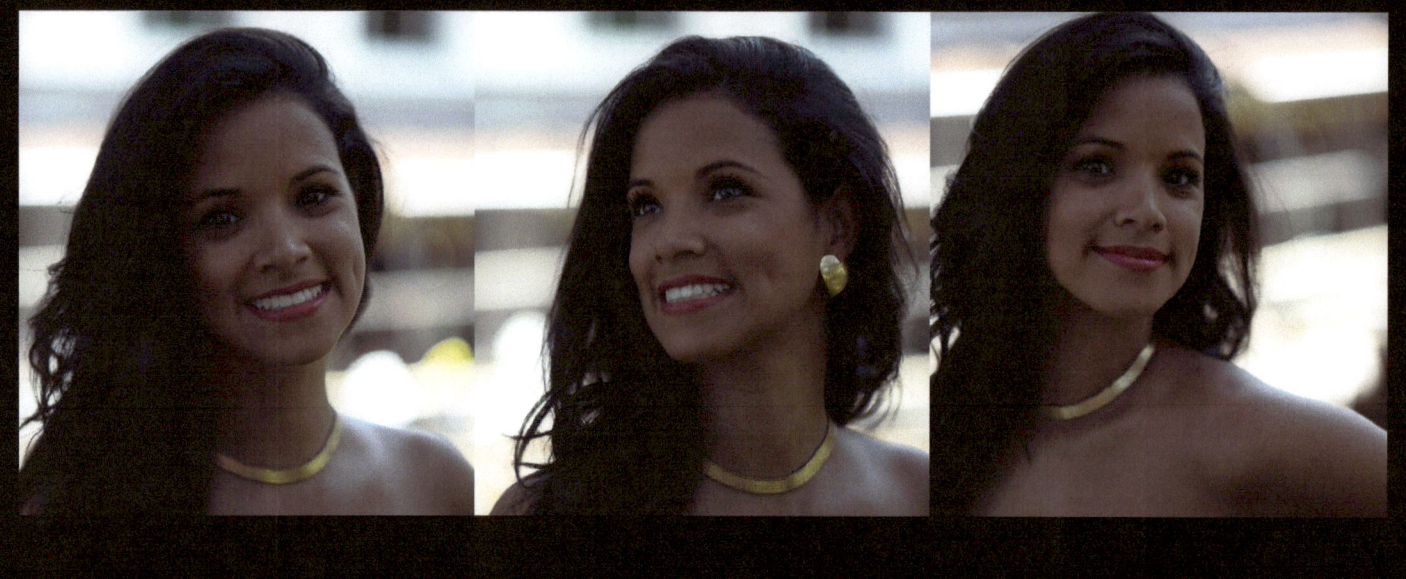
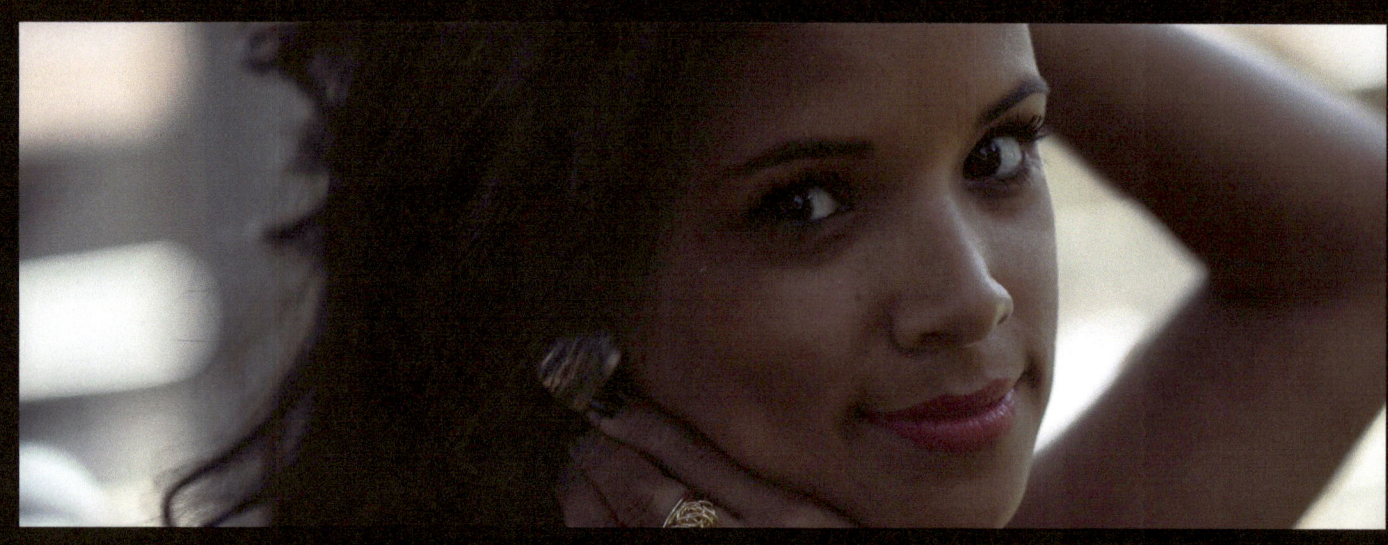
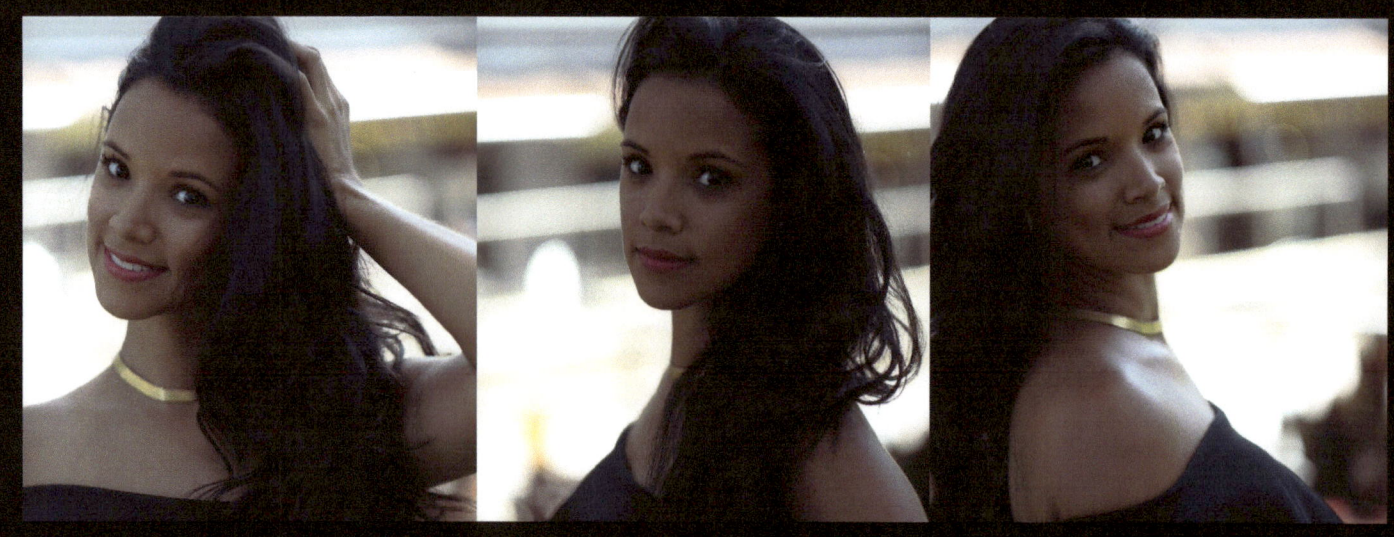

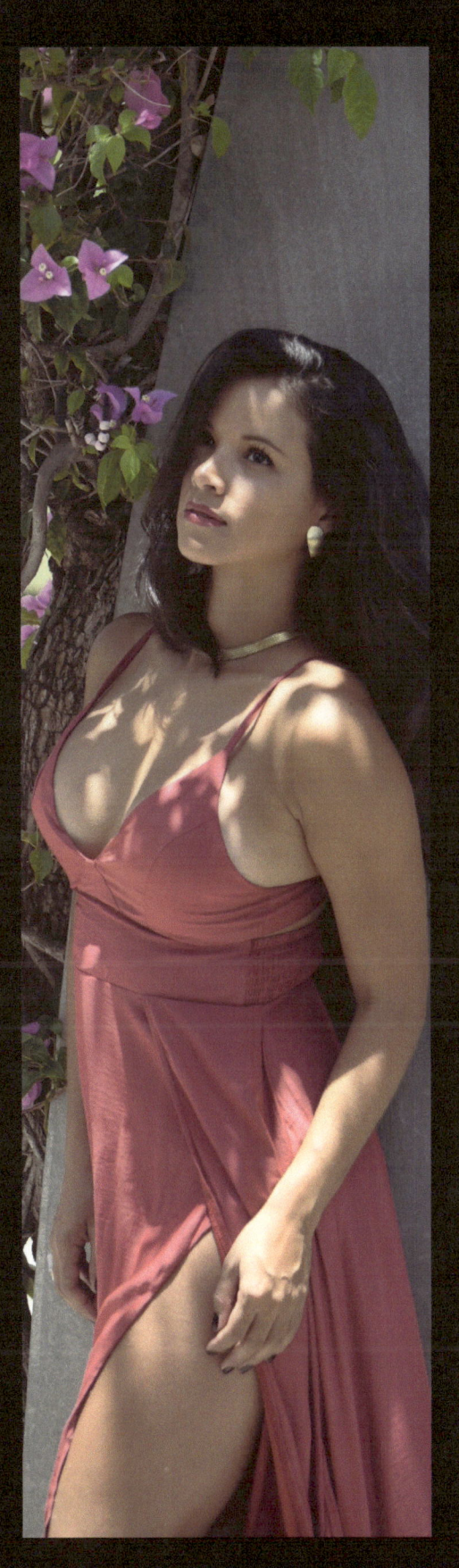
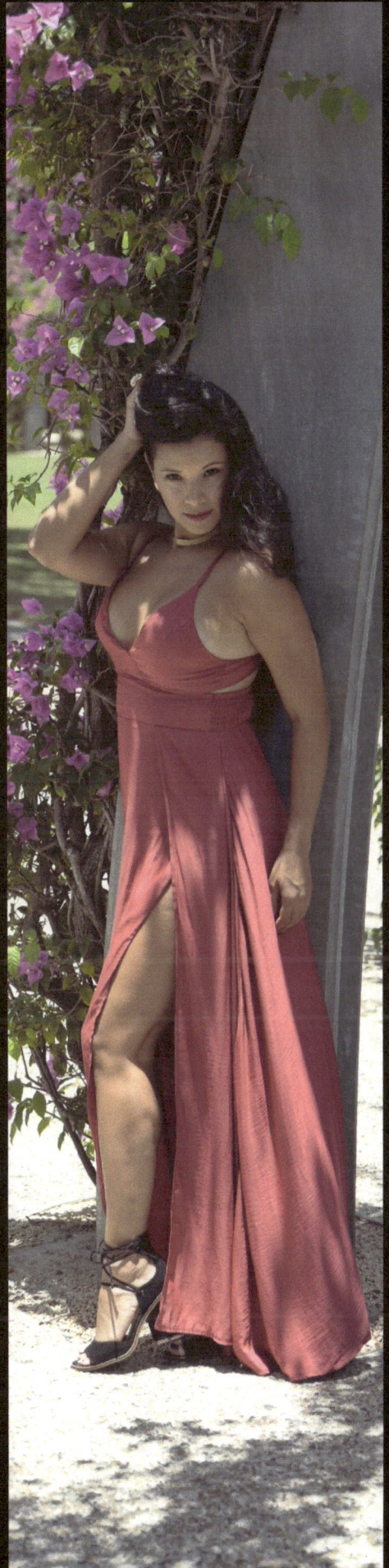
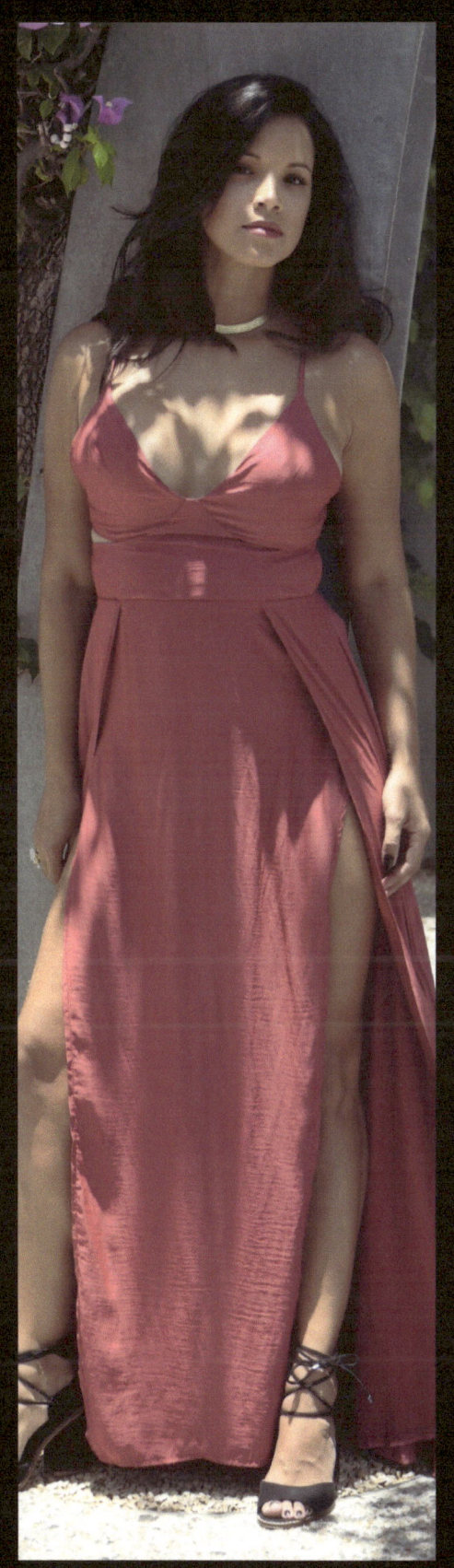

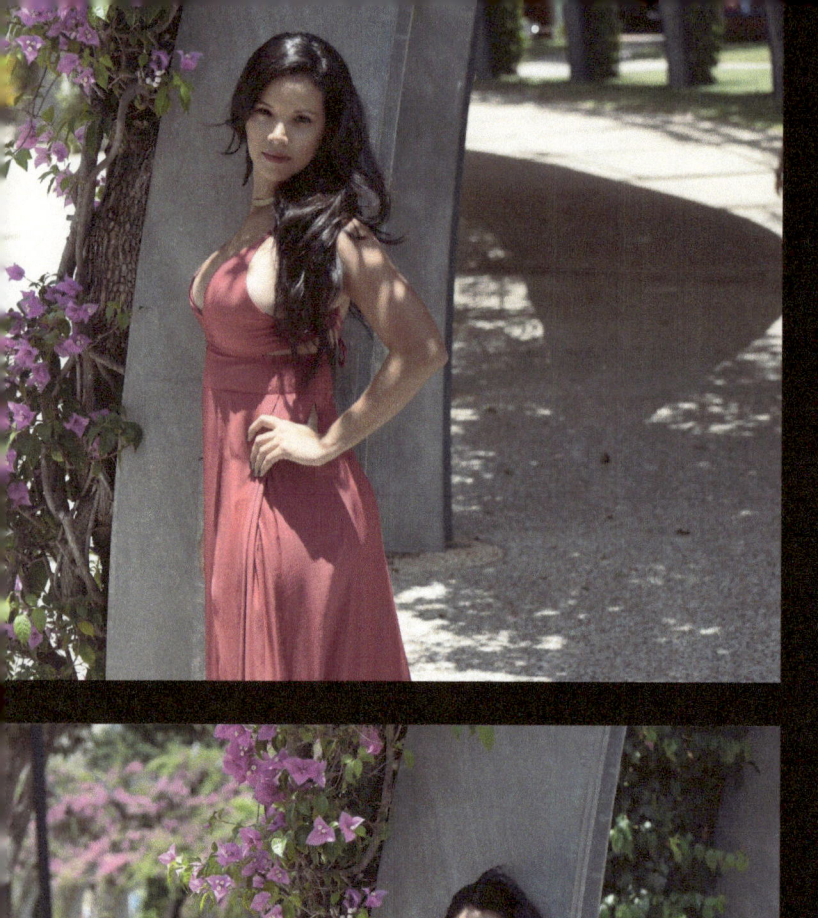
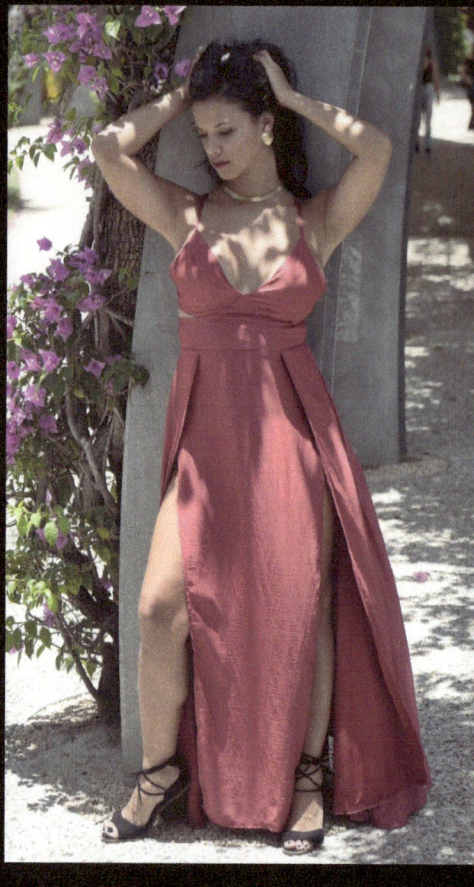
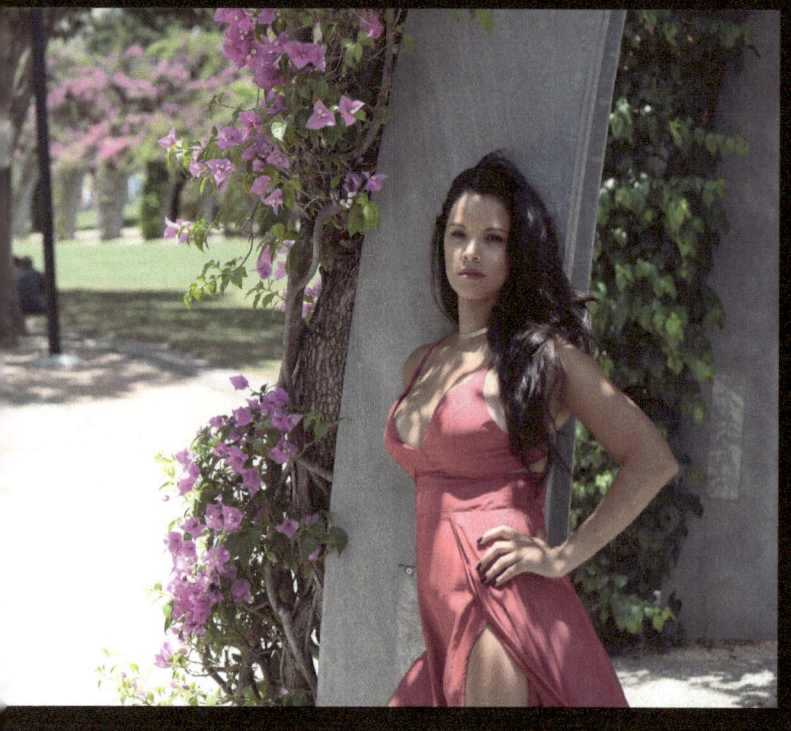
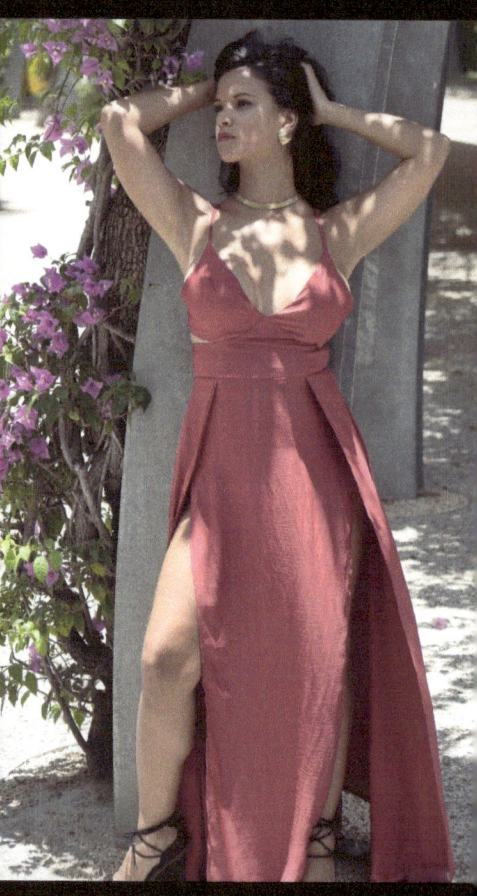
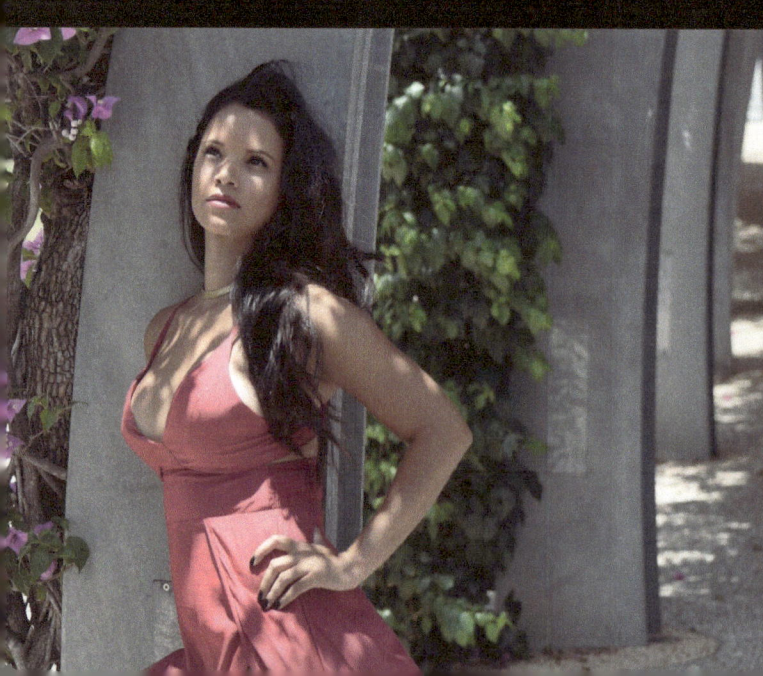

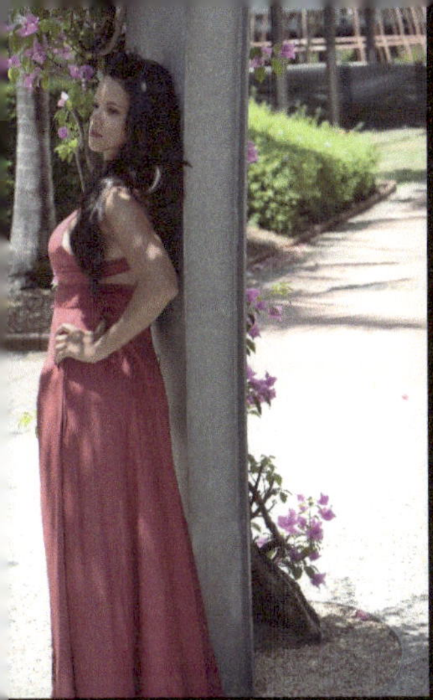

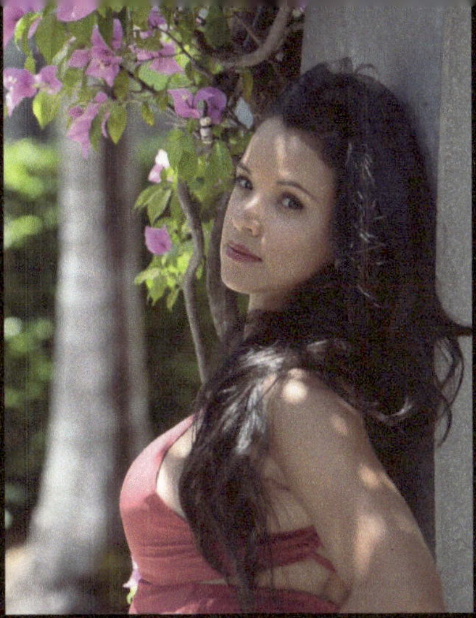

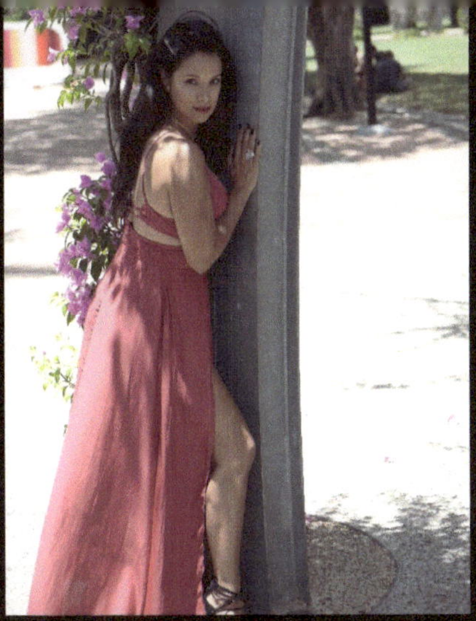

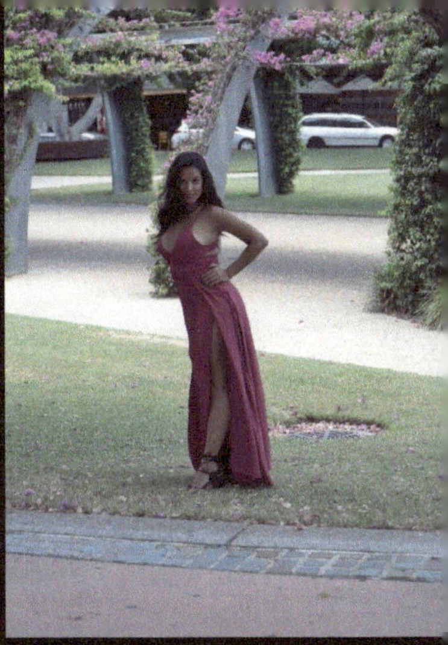

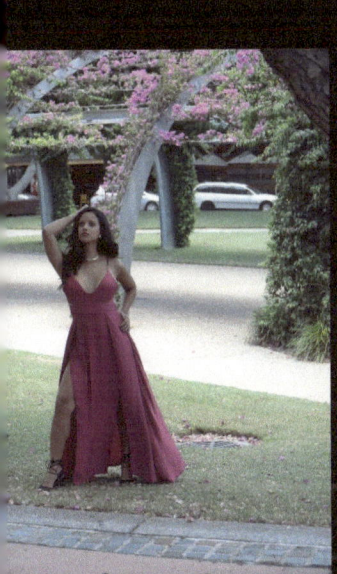
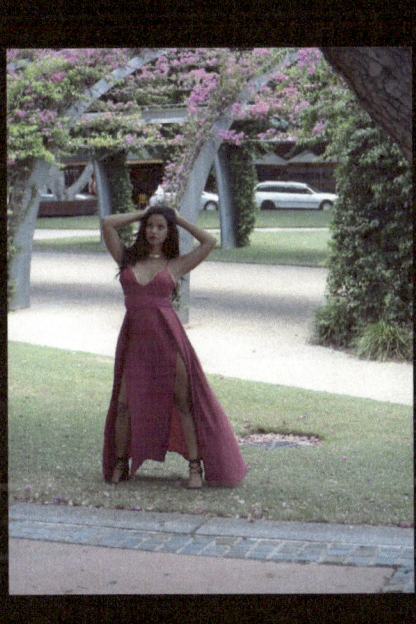
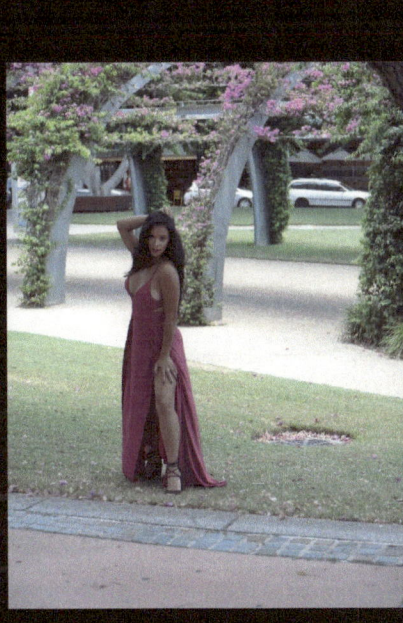
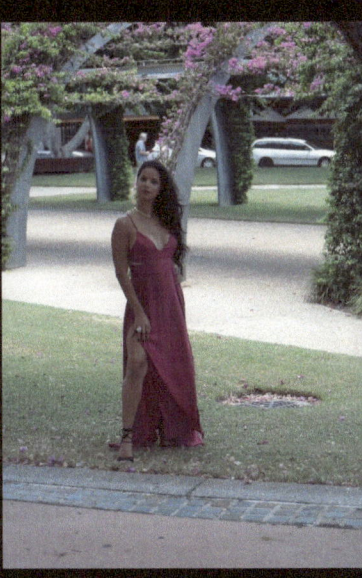
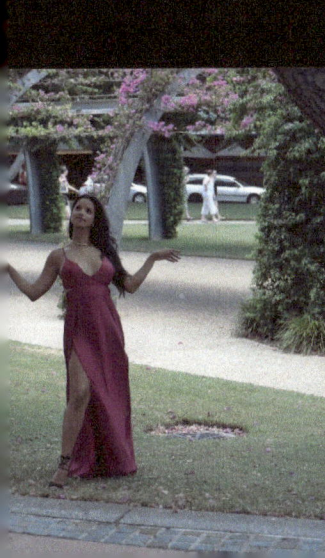
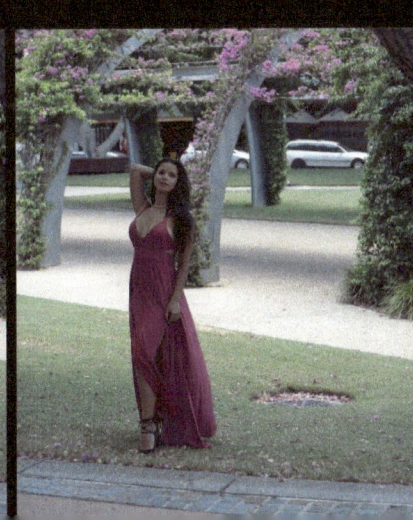
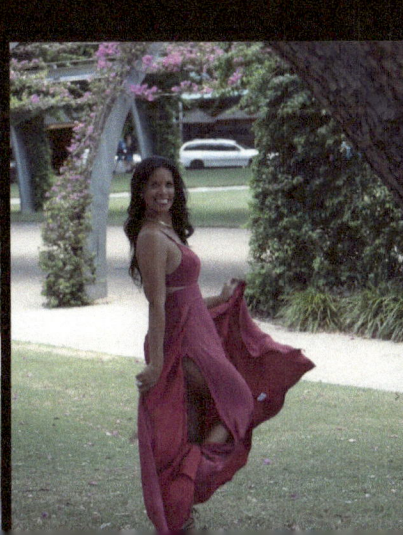
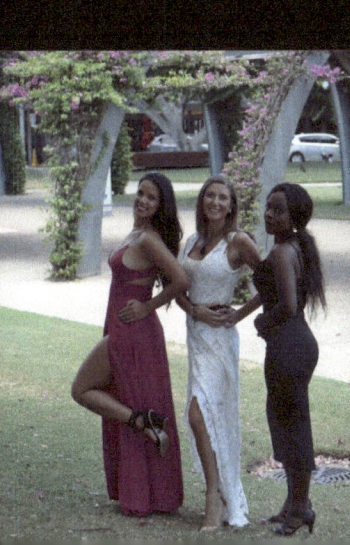

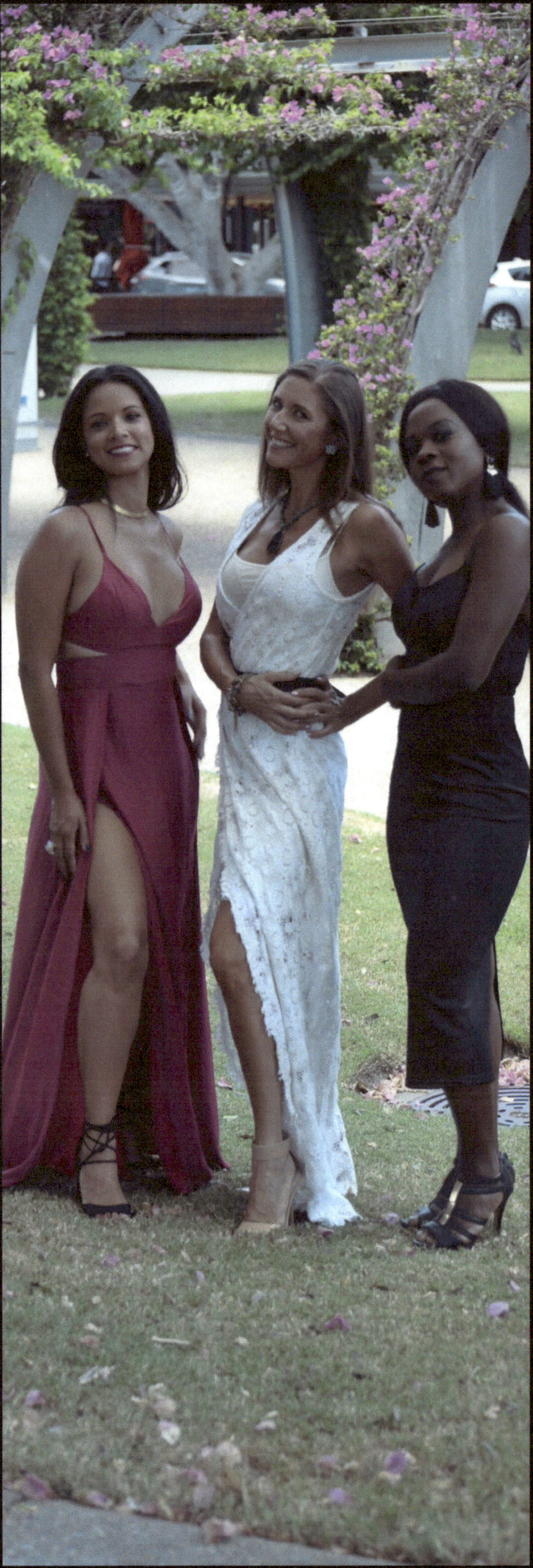

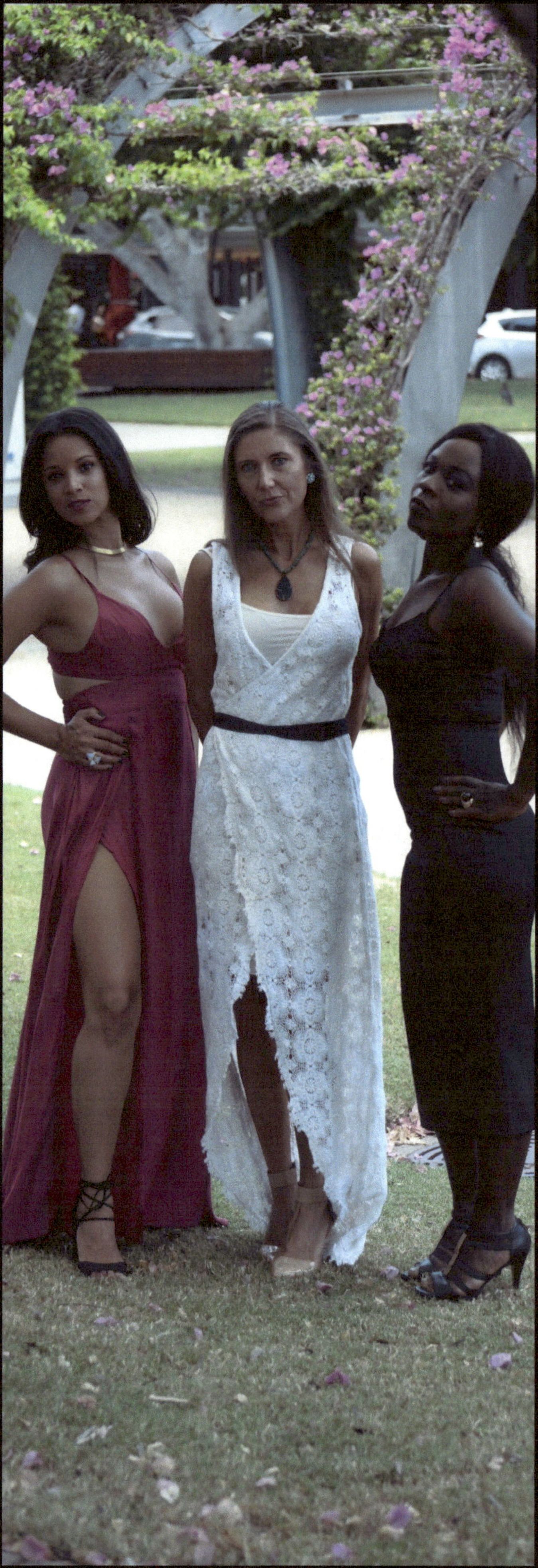

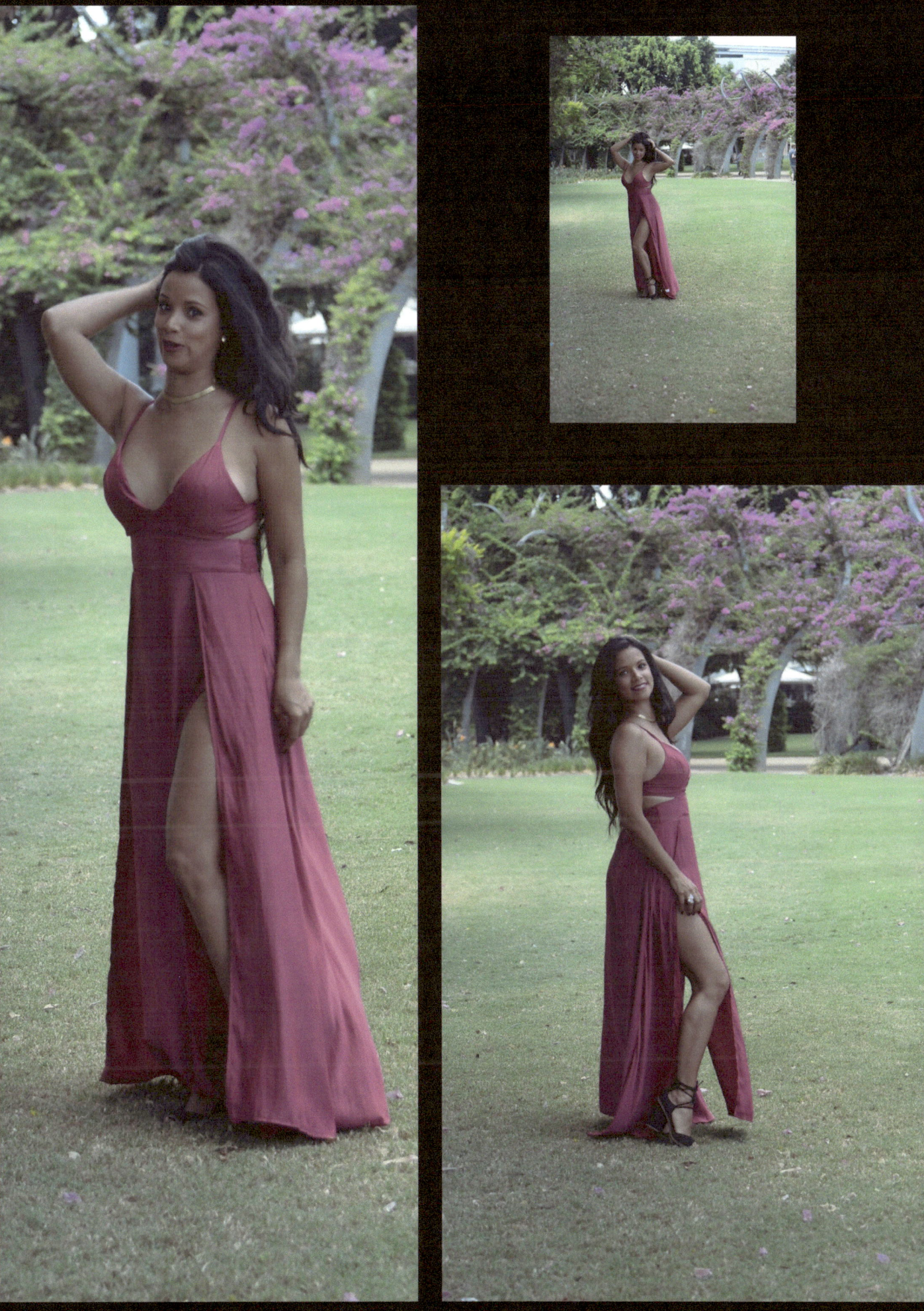

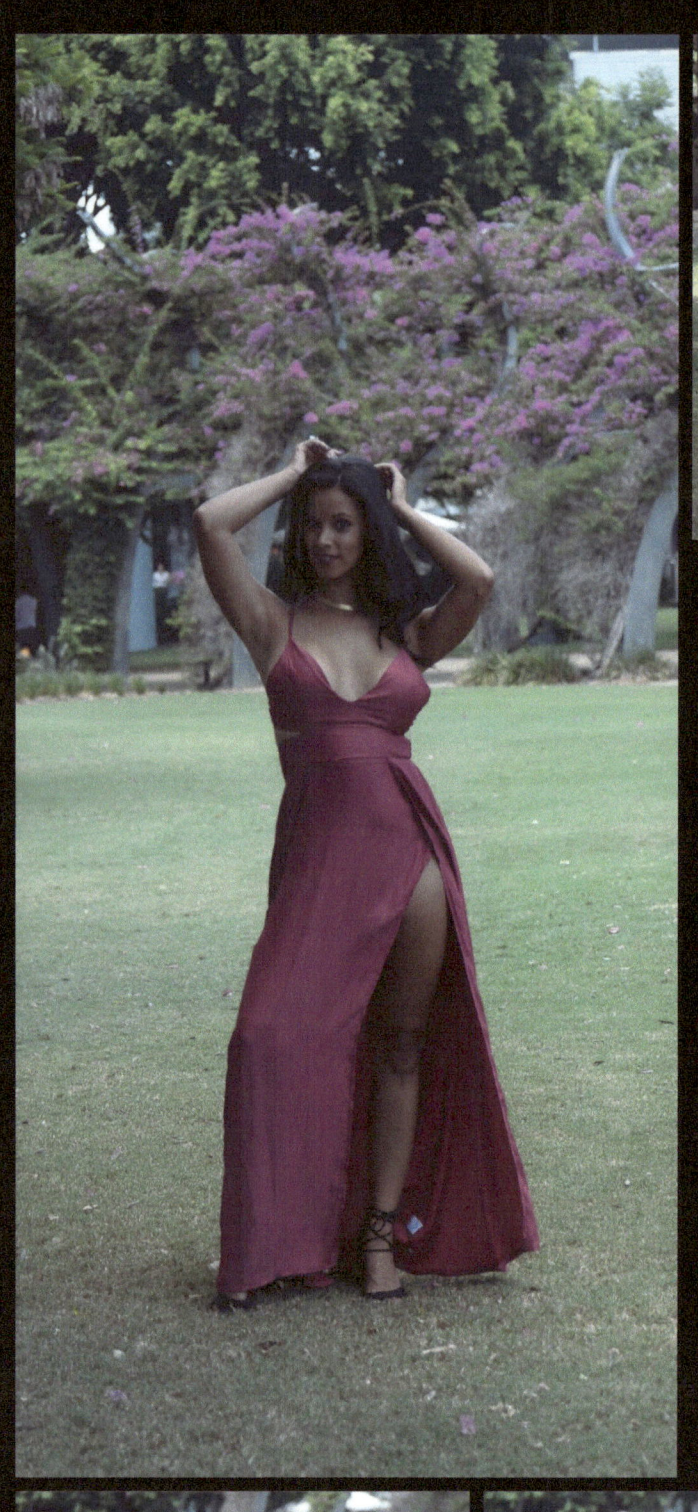
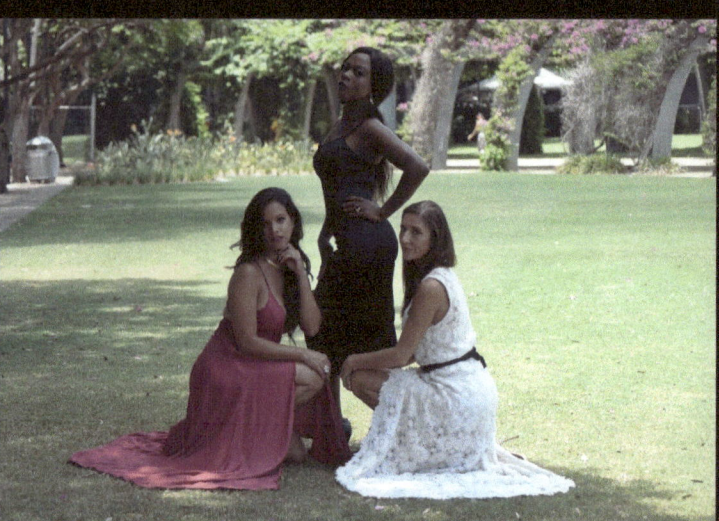
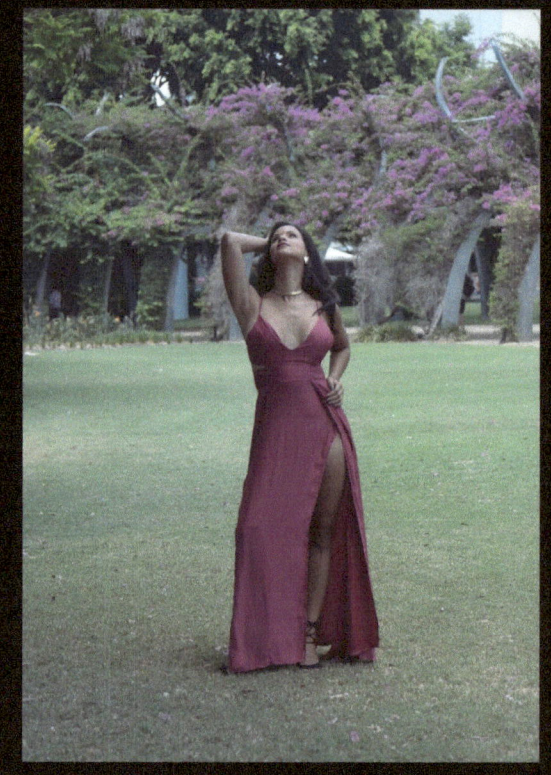
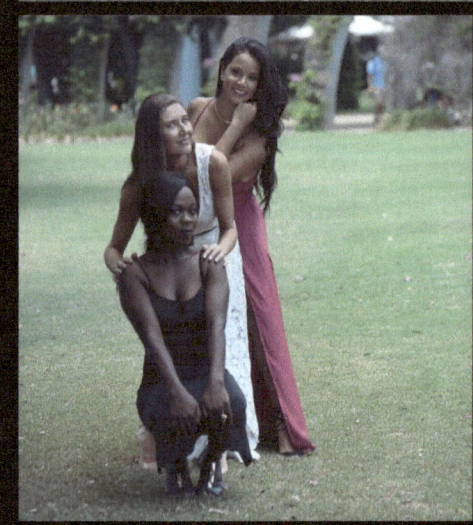
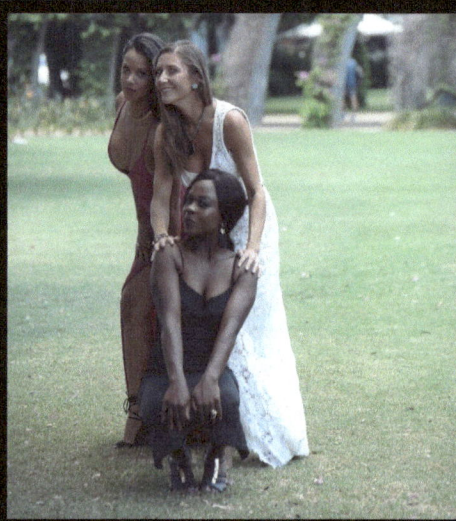
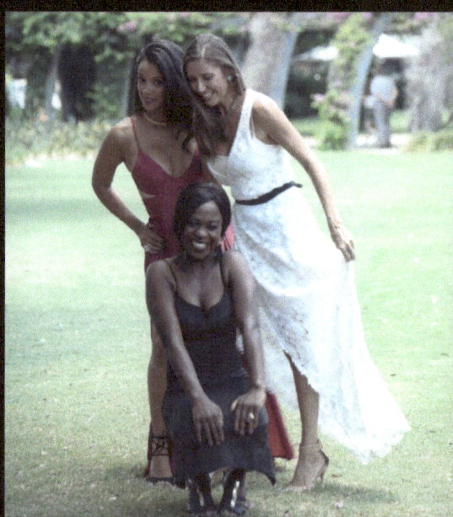

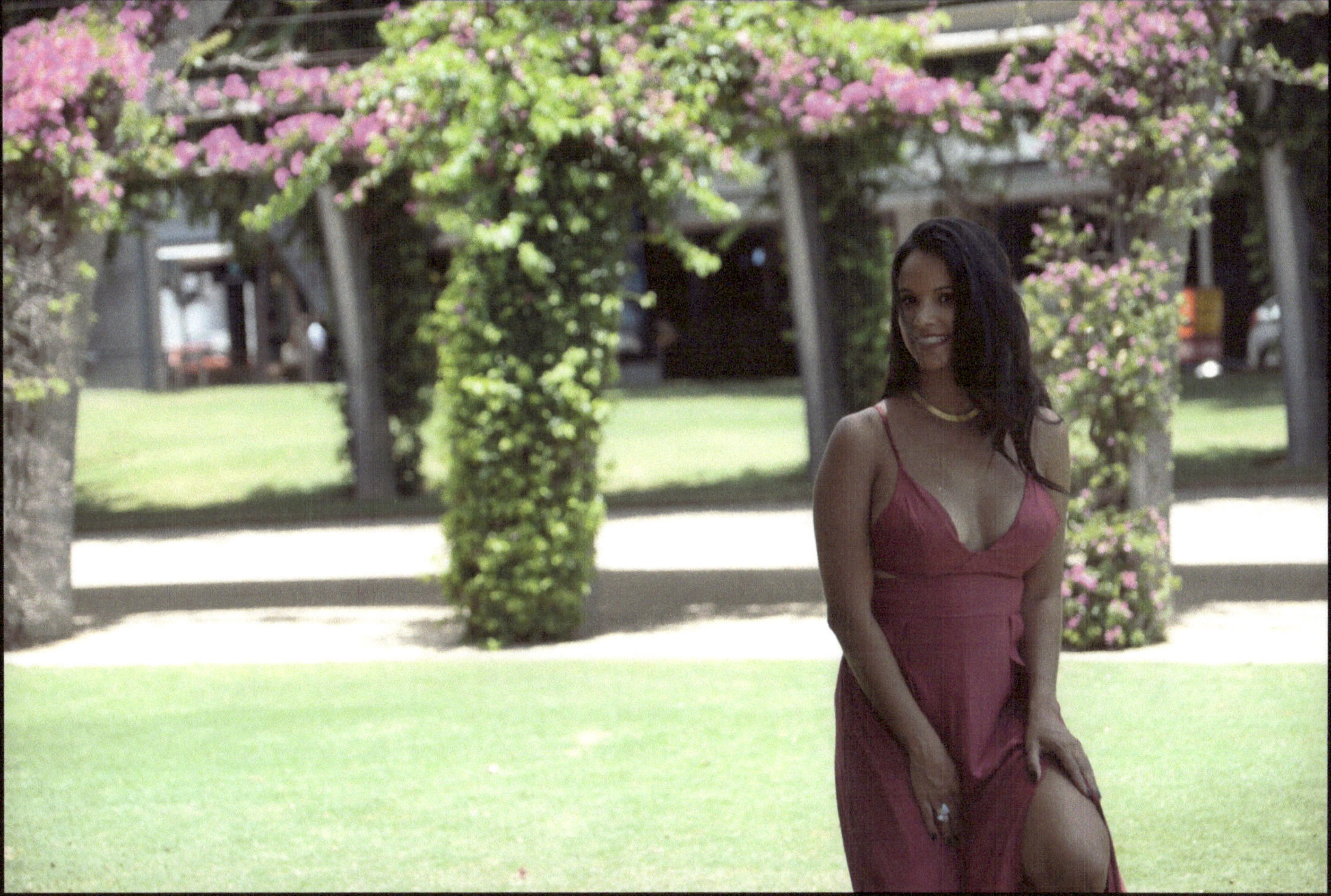

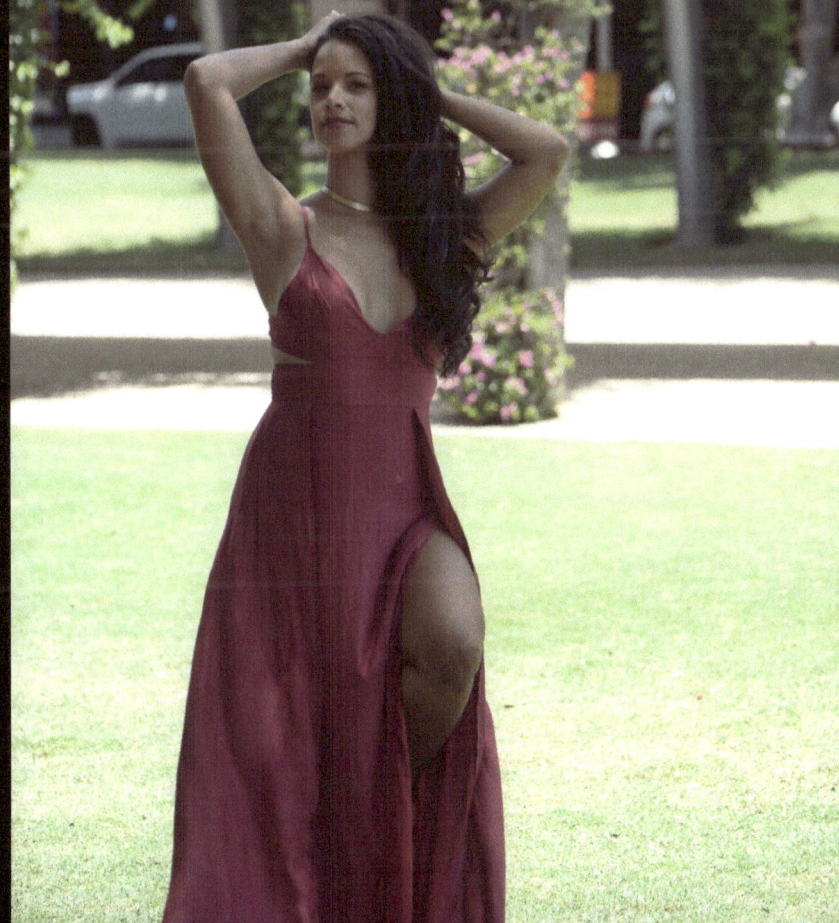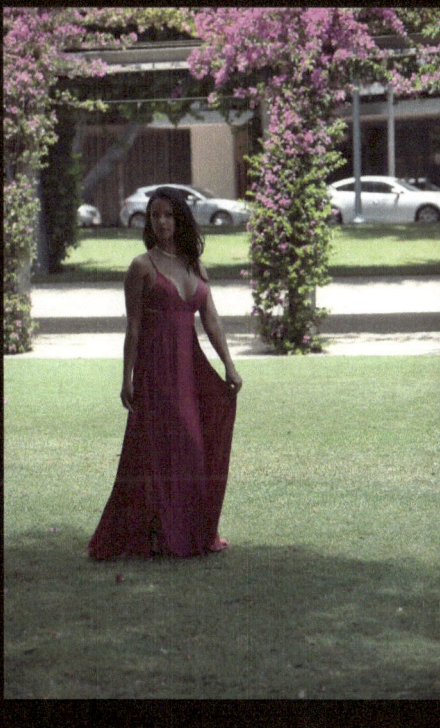

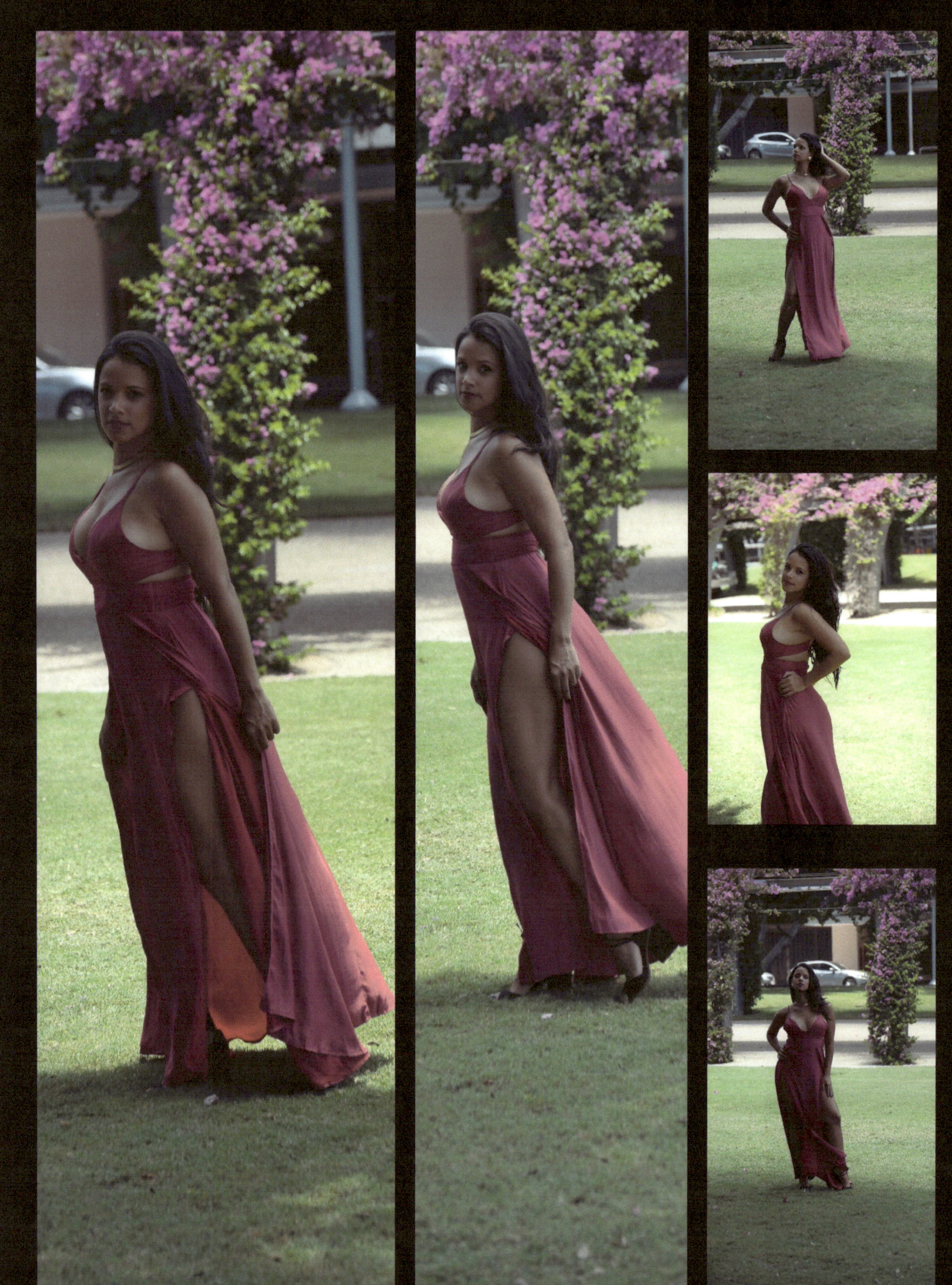

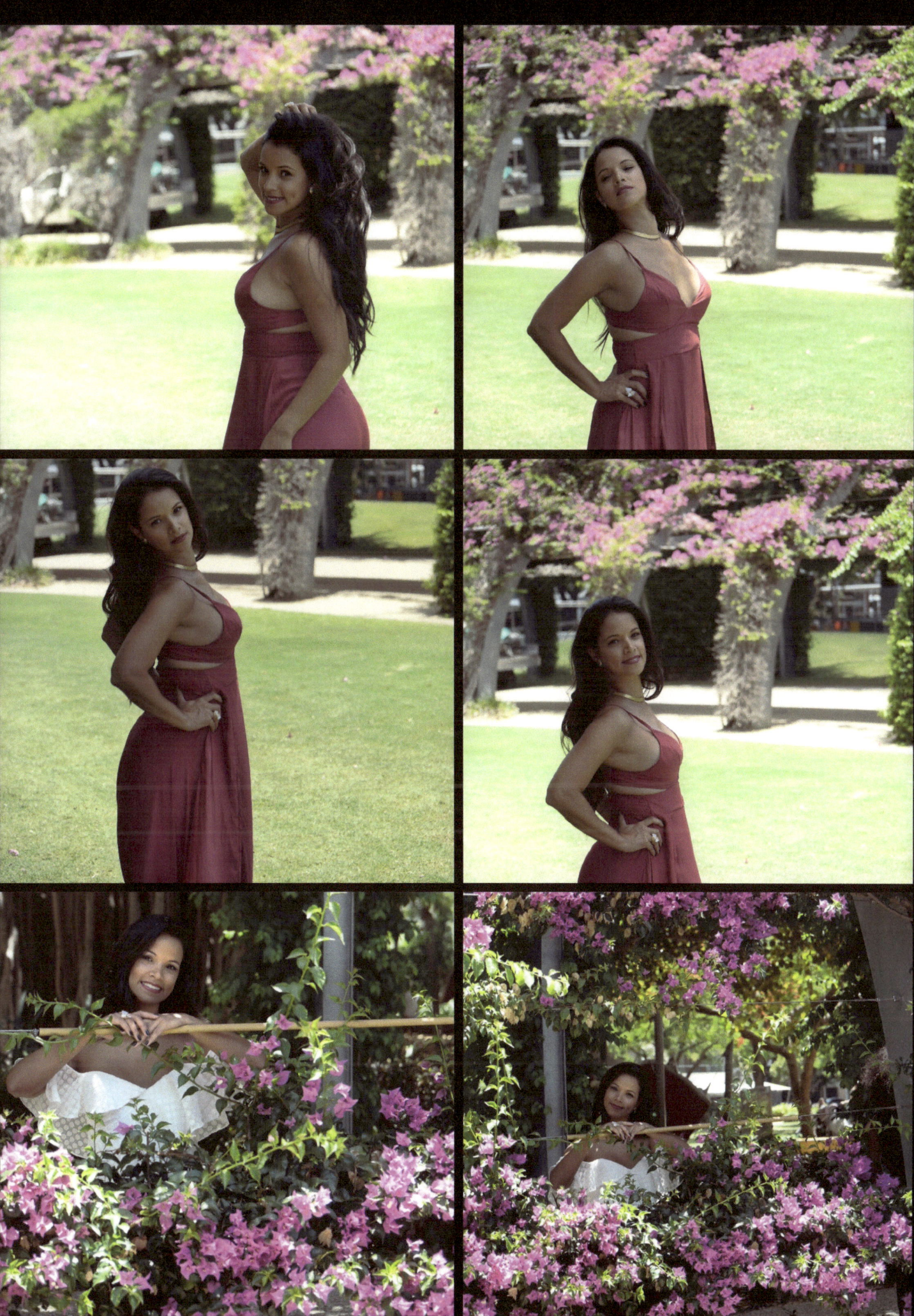

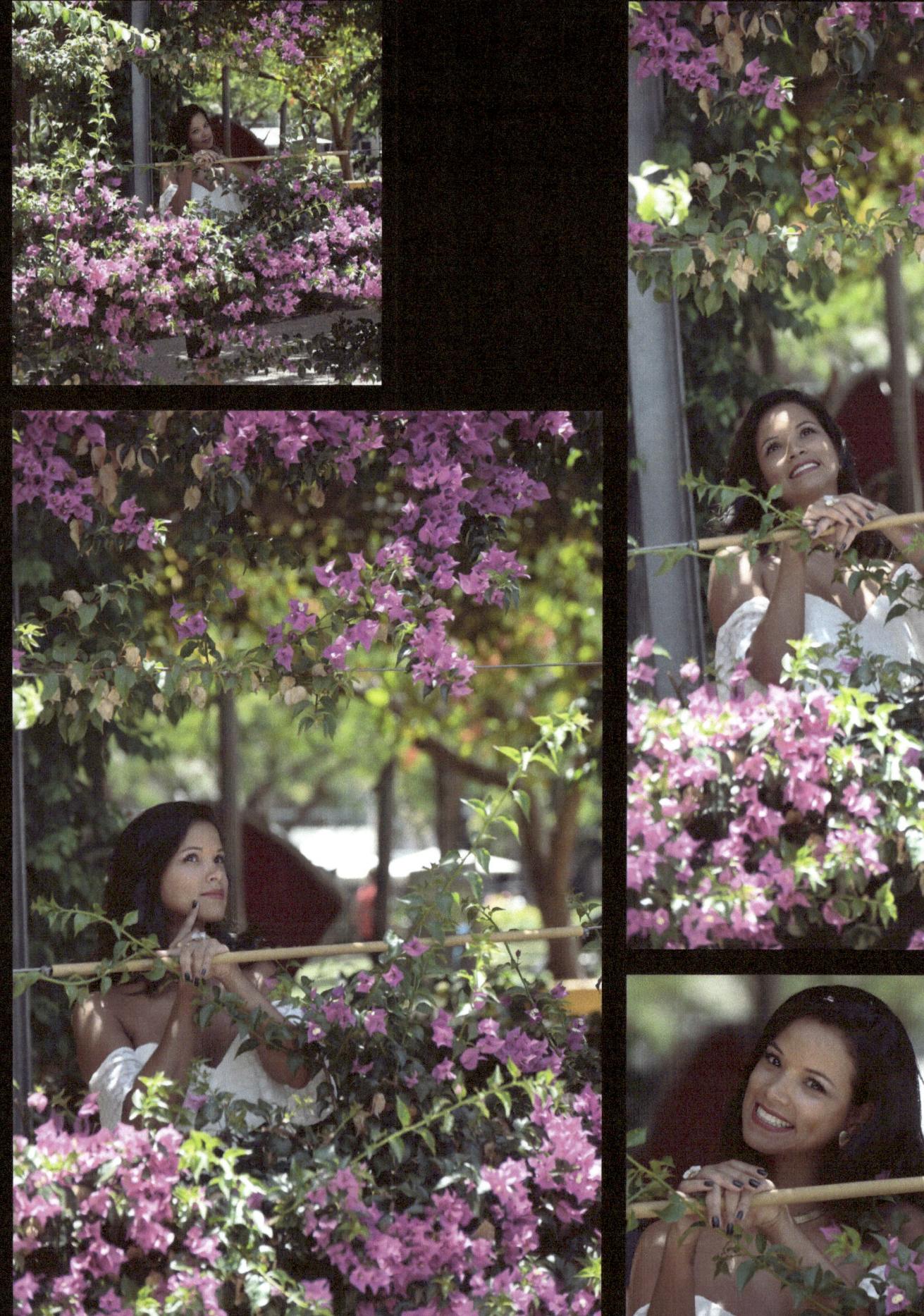

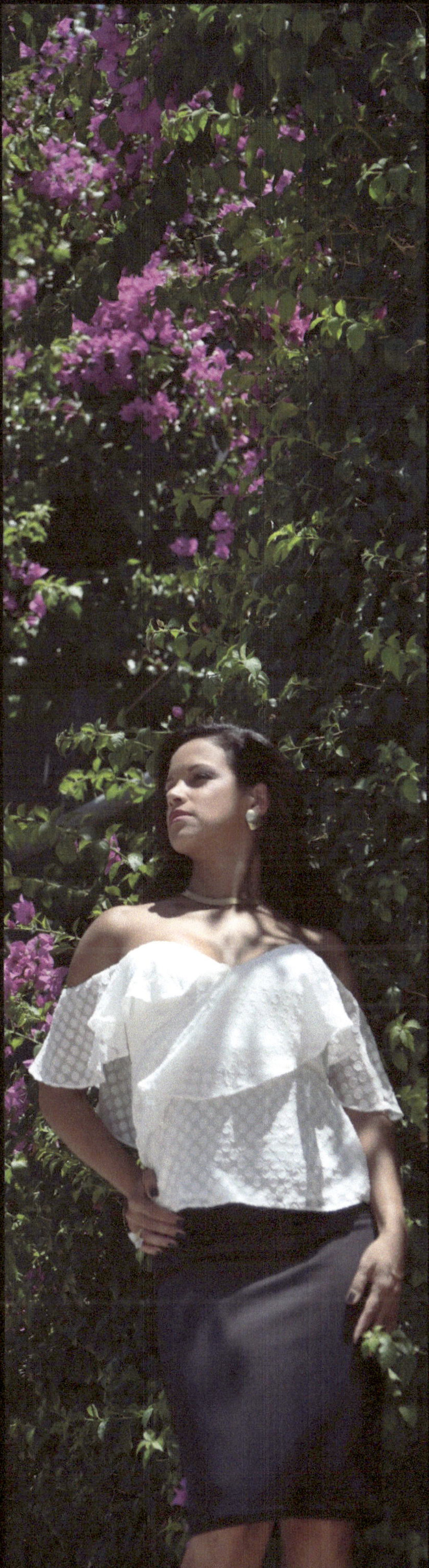

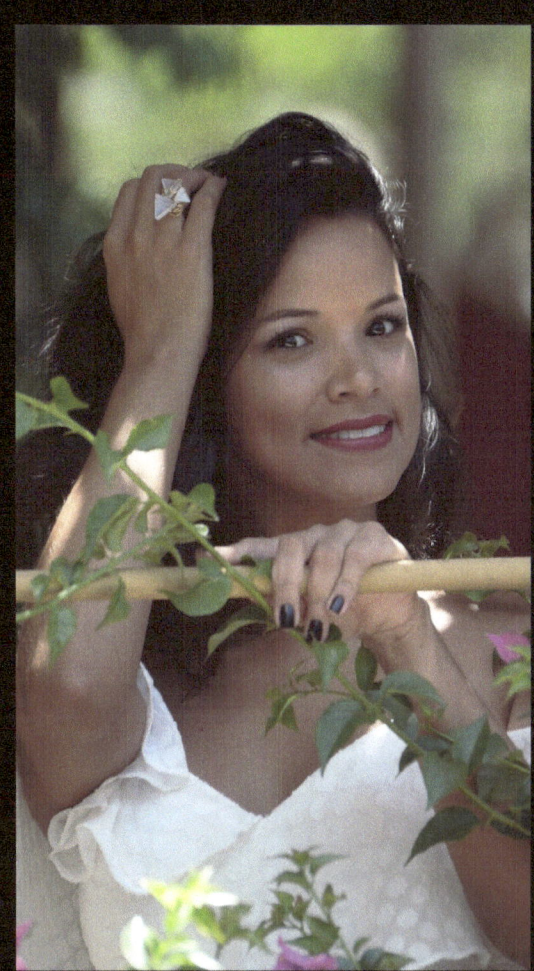
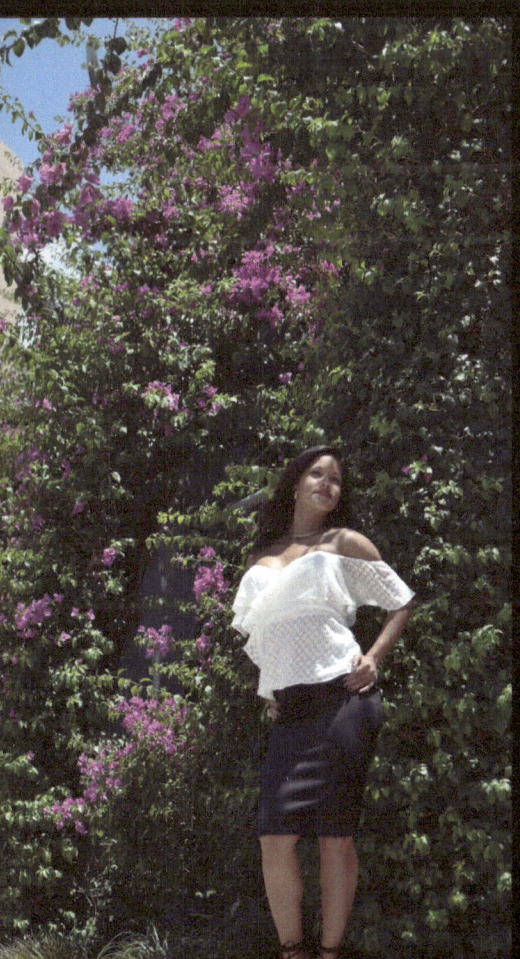

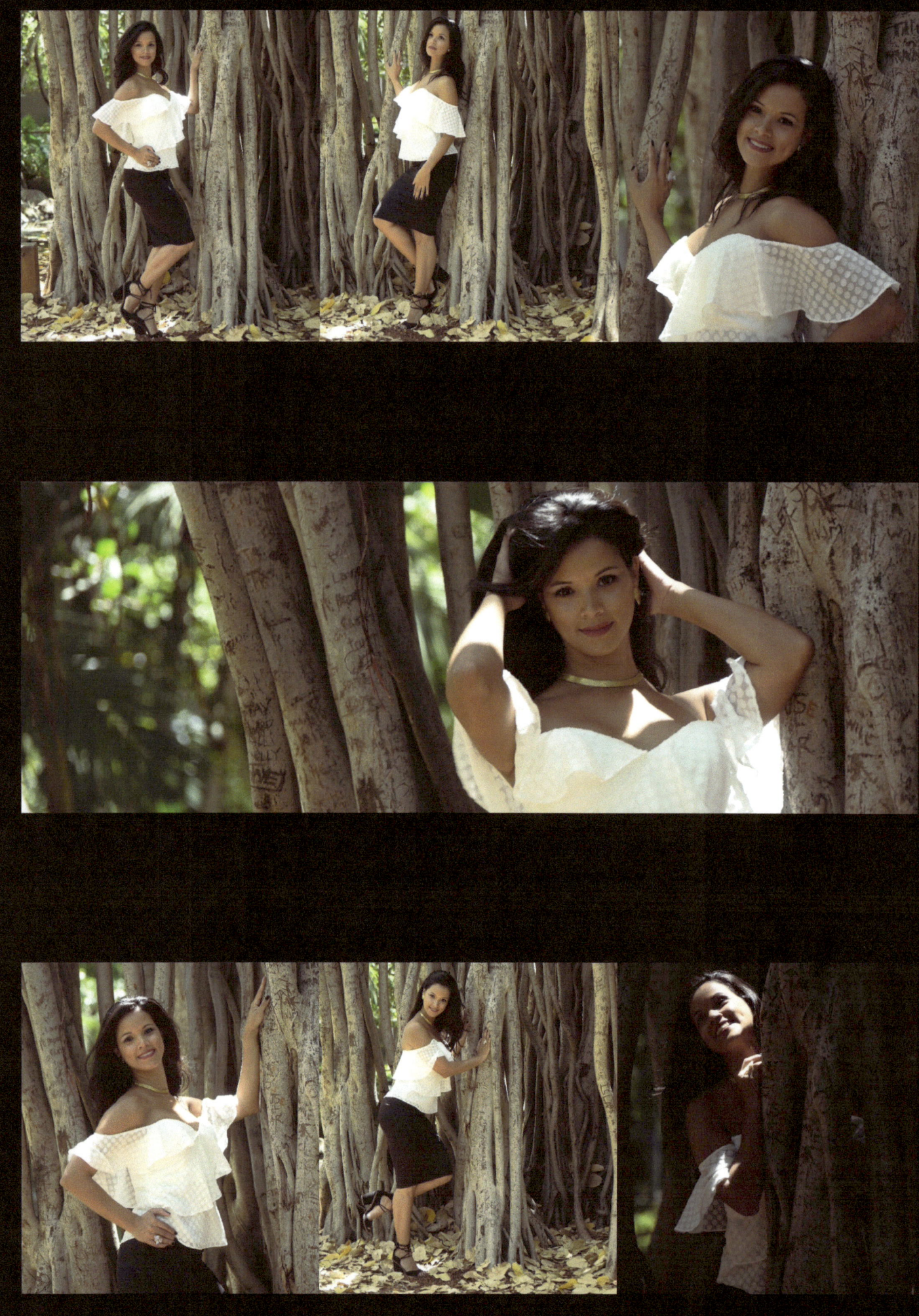

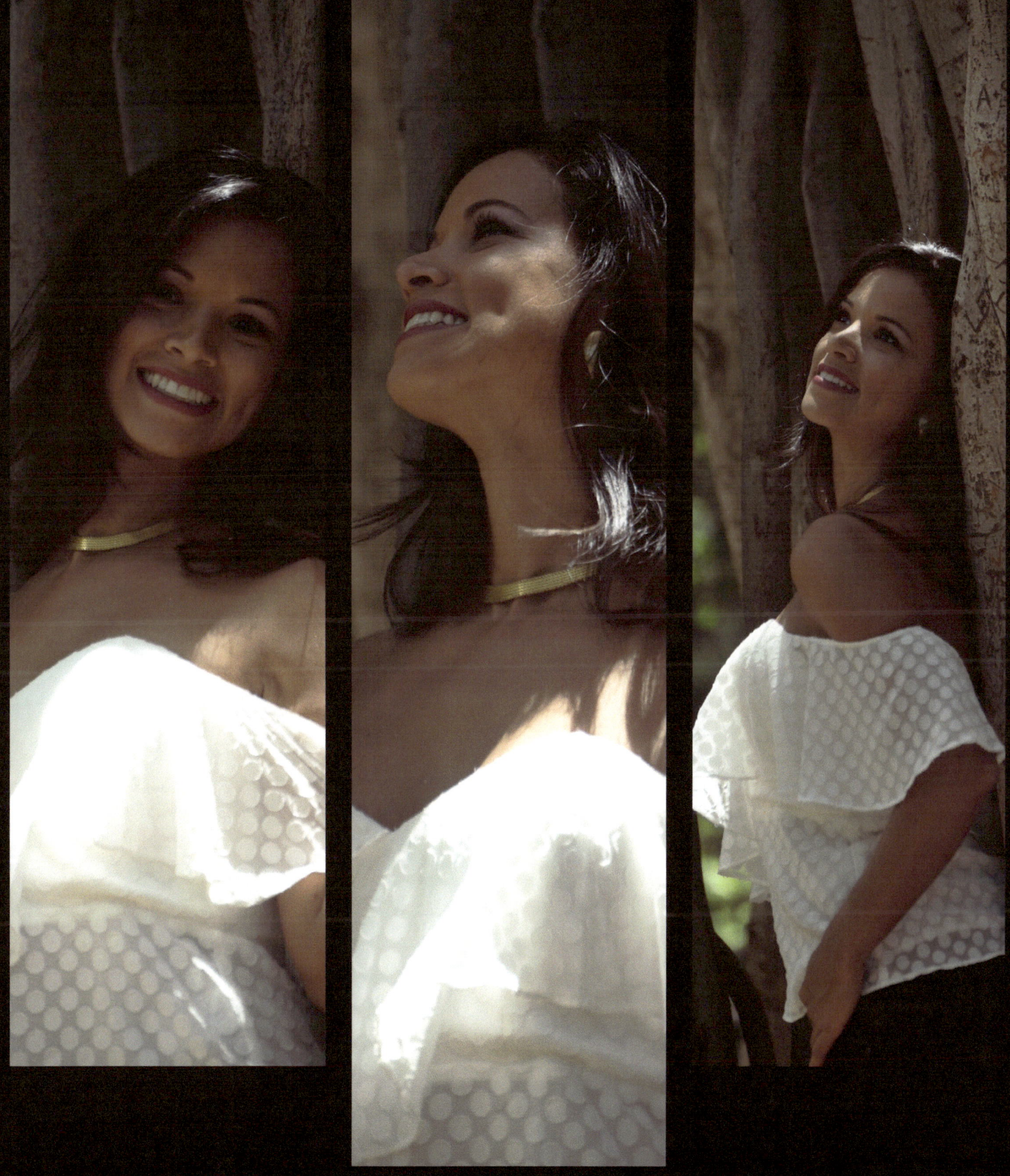

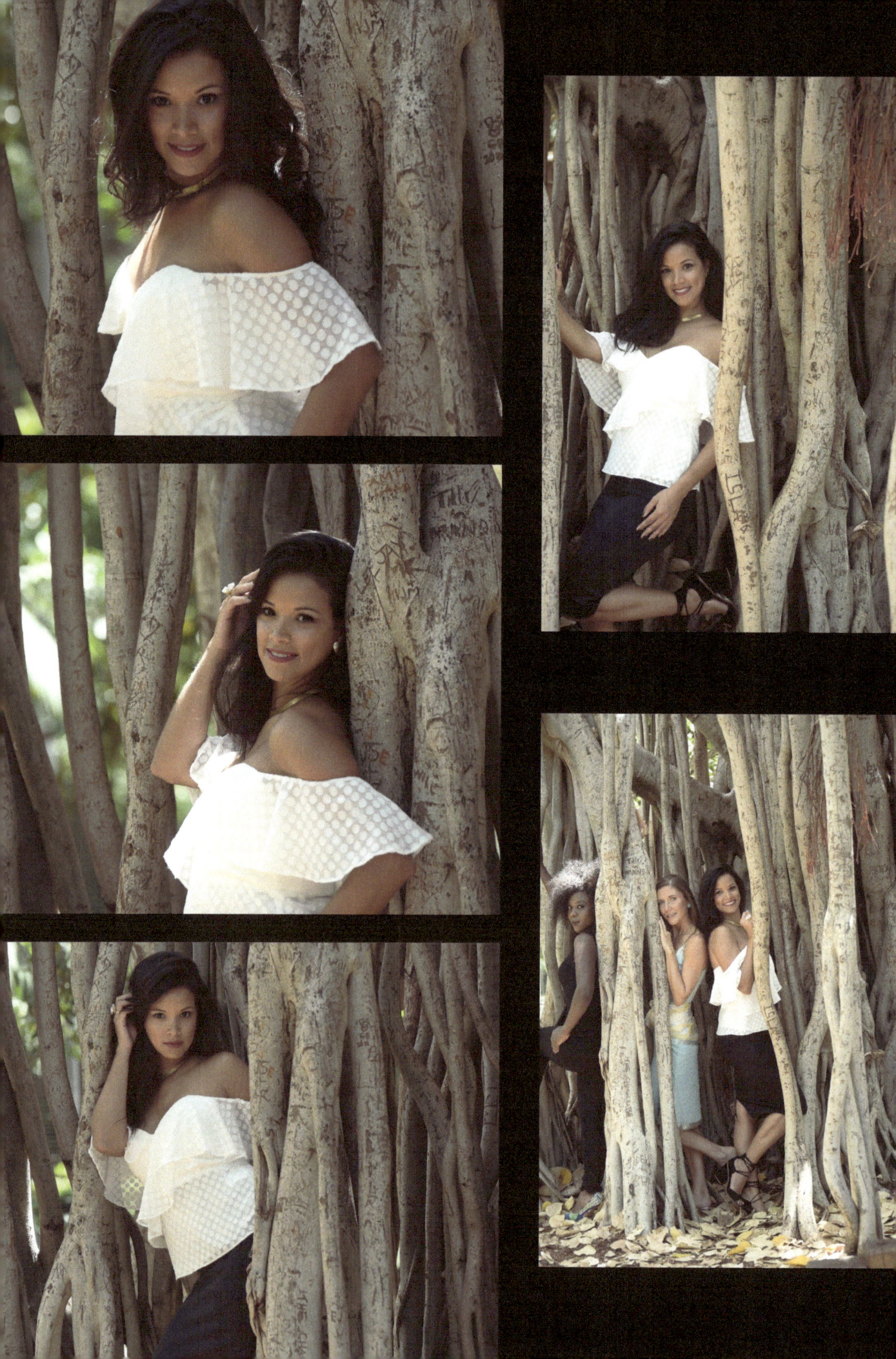

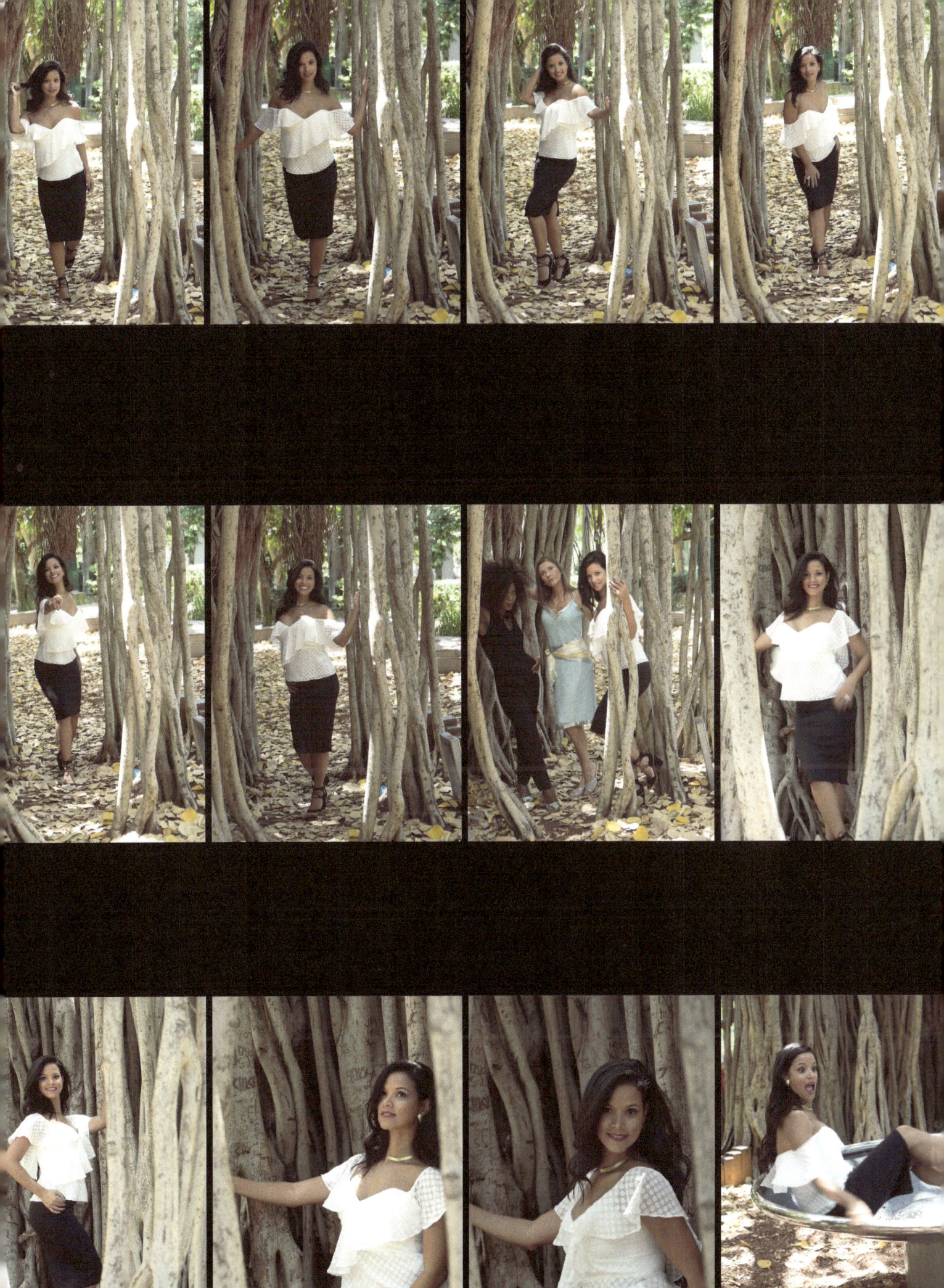

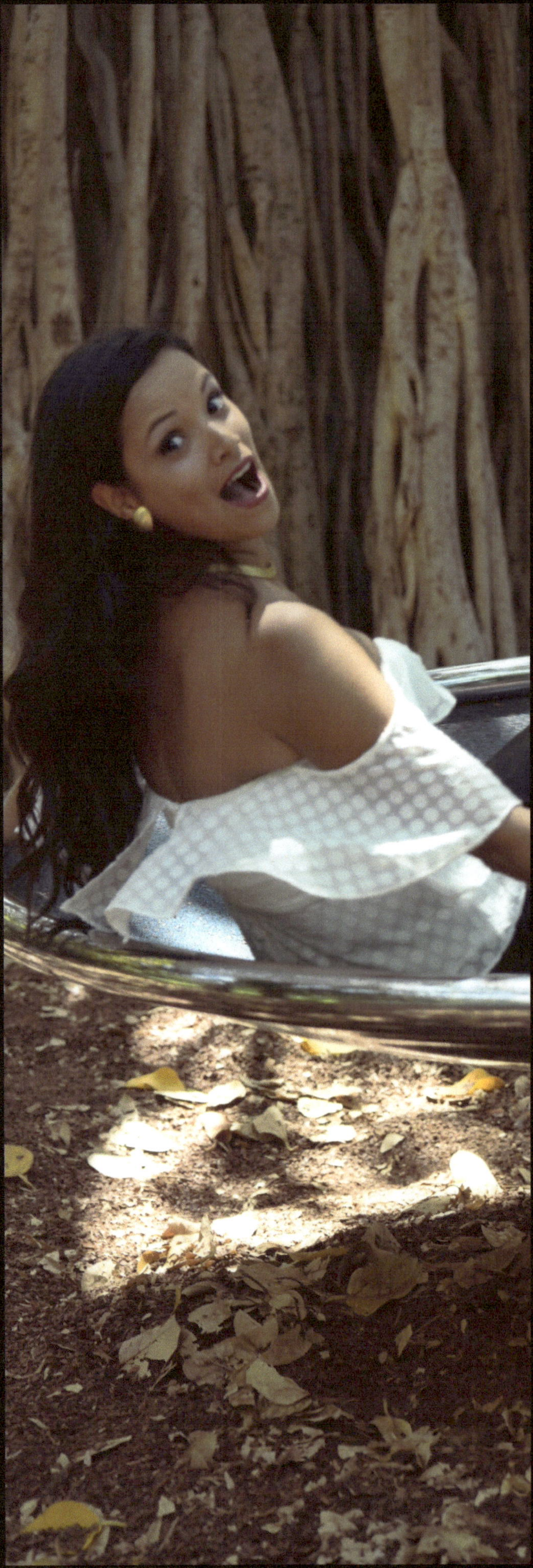

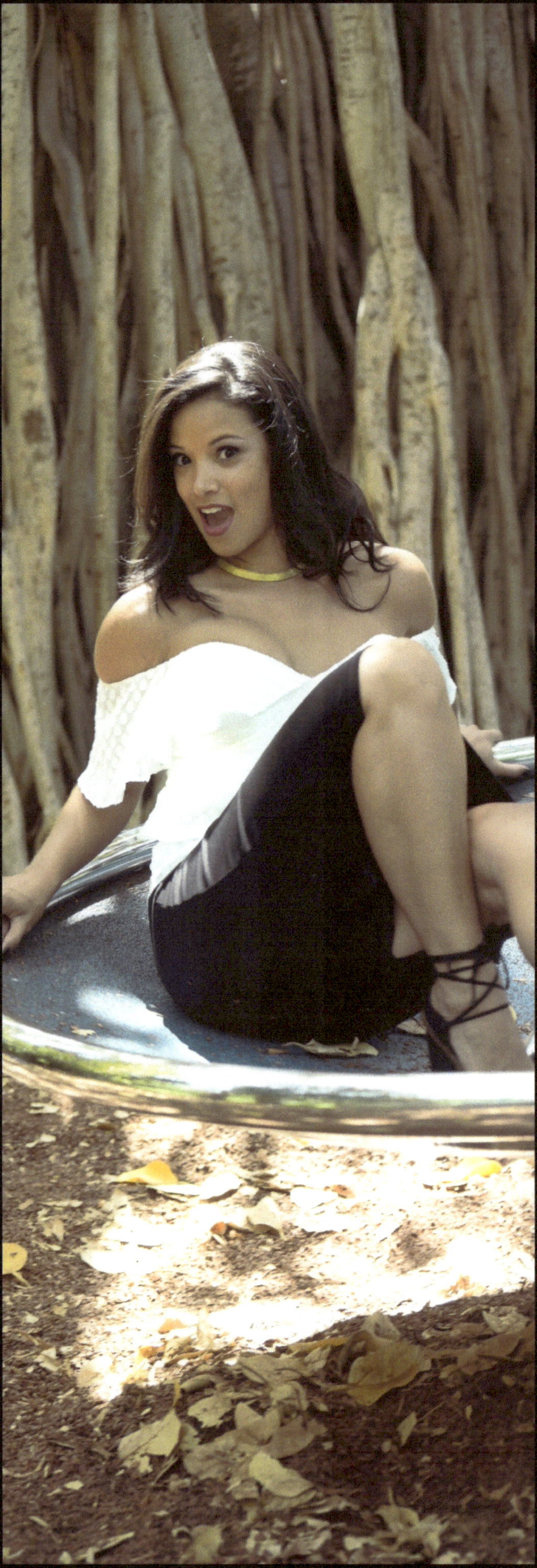

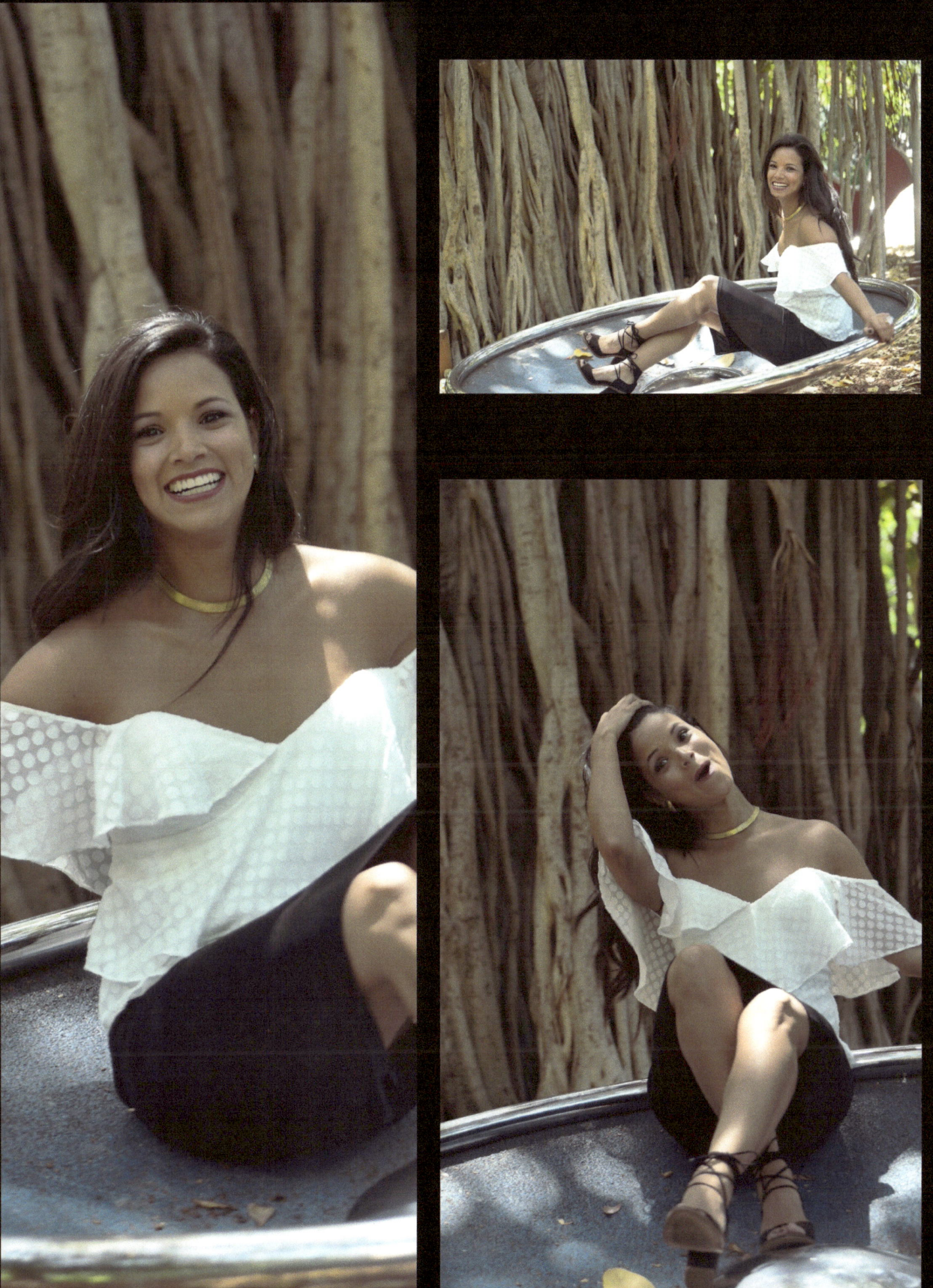

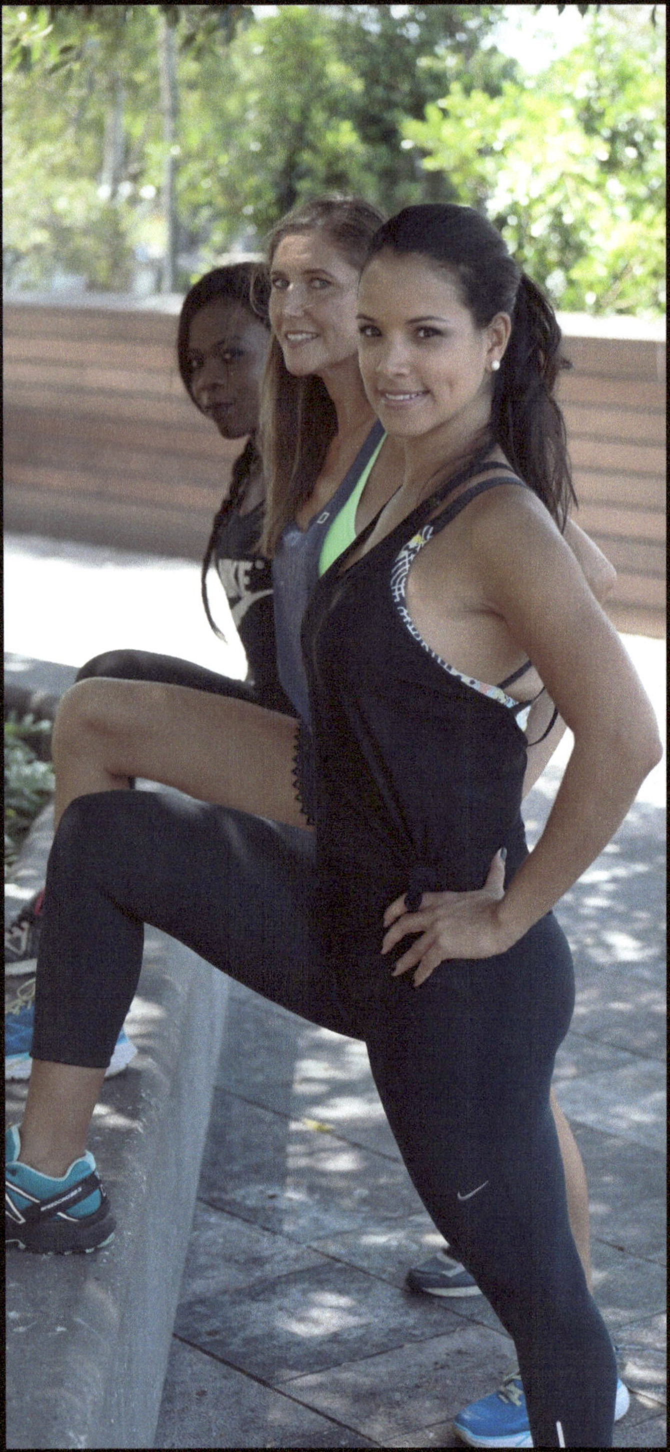

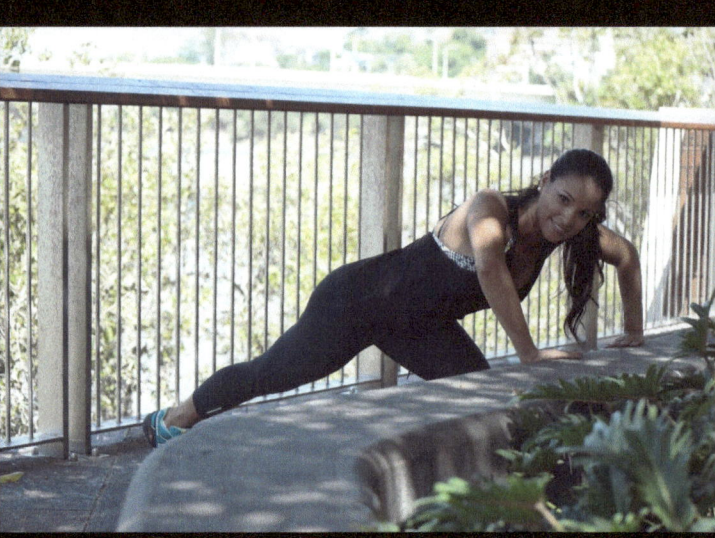
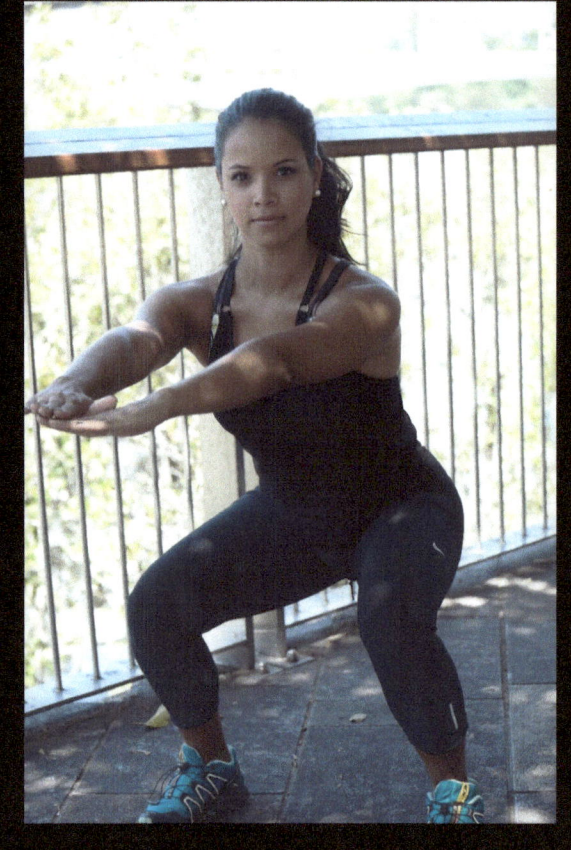
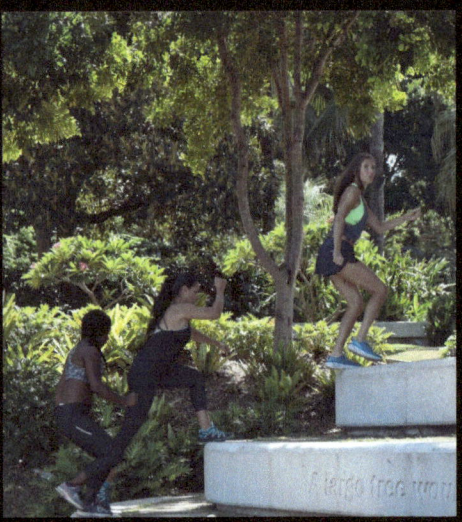
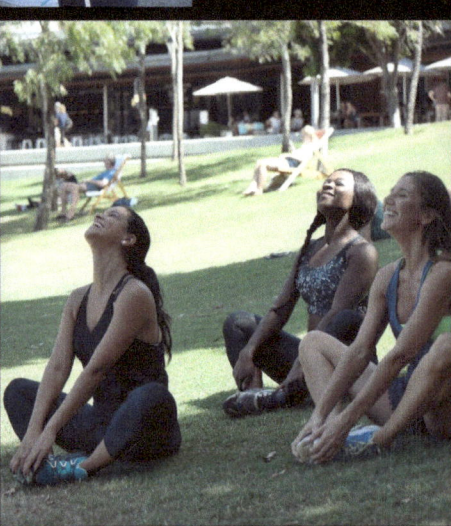
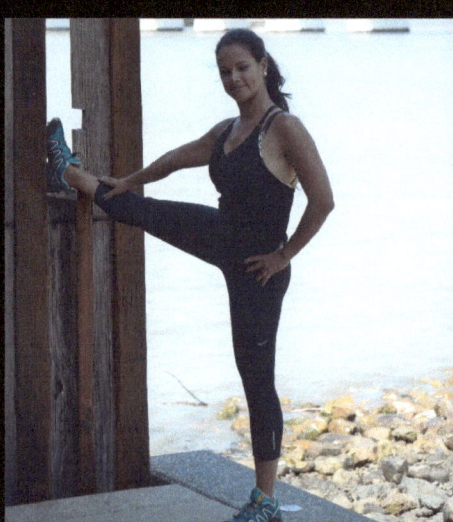

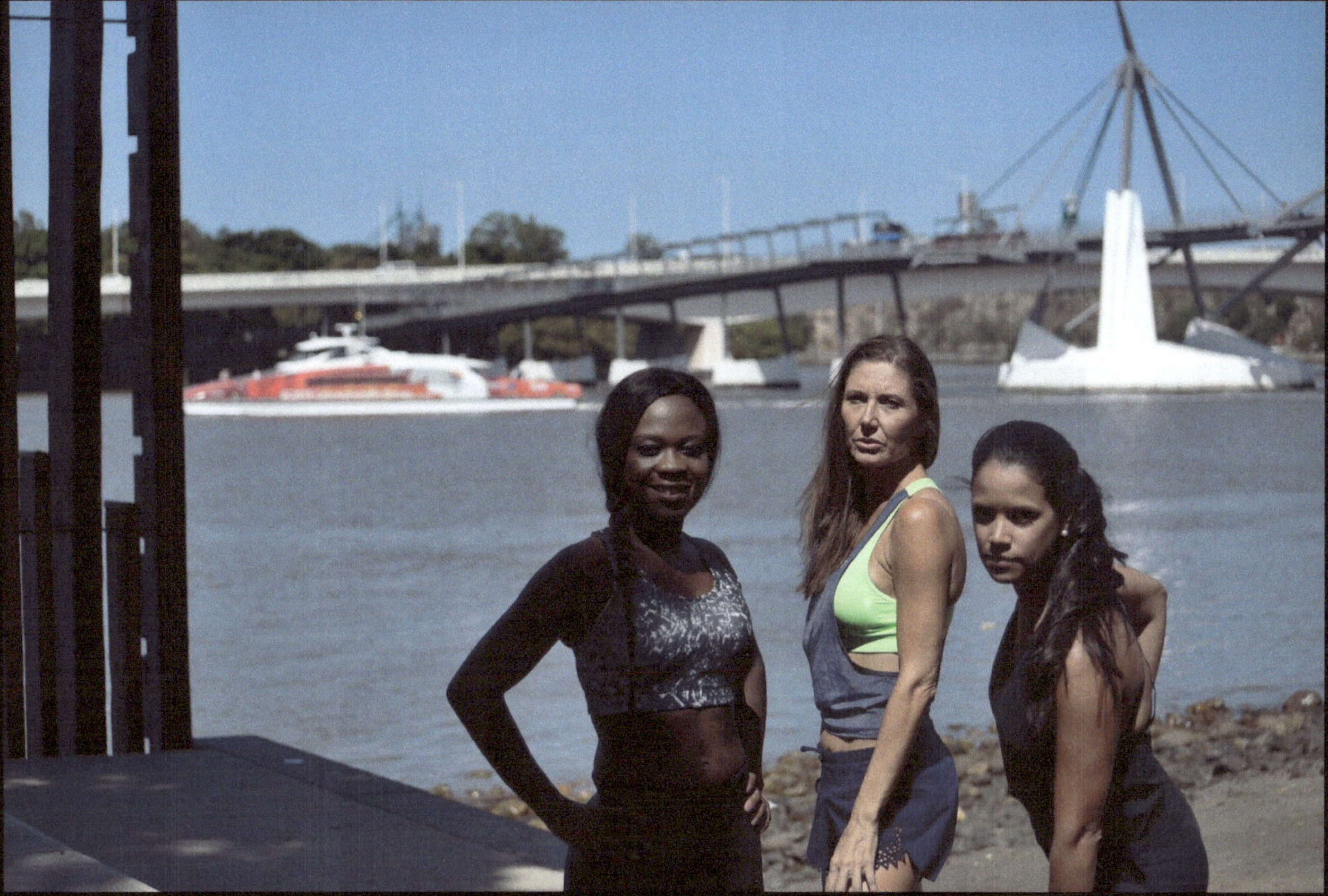

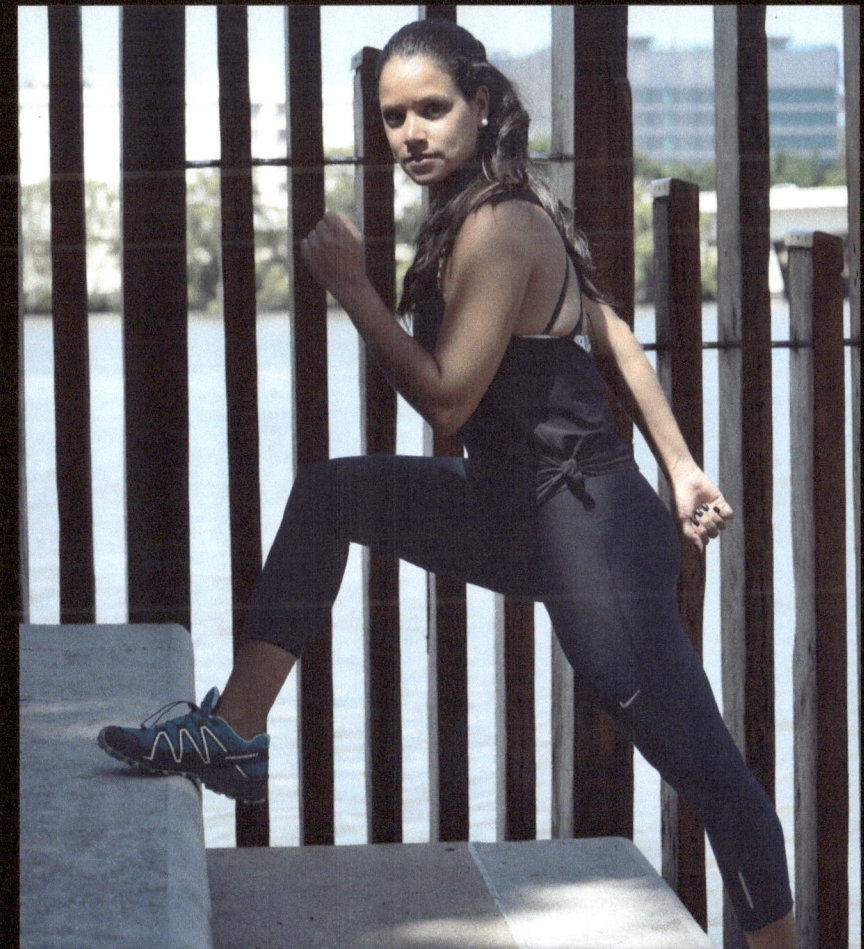
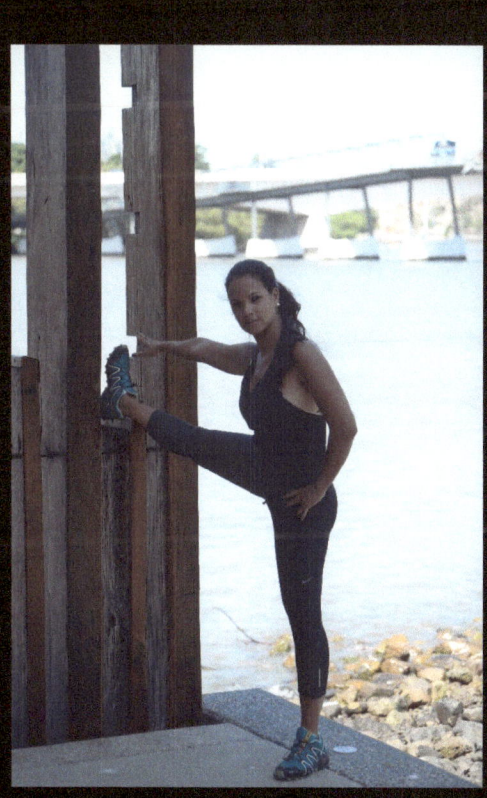

The thirty pages of colour photos you have just viewed is the Flip Portfolio for Eillyn Paz.

This is the standard sized Flip Portfolio, A standard size Flip Portfolio is any page number up to a maximum of thirty pages.

You also can have a standard Flip Portfolio for as little as Au$140.00. That includes the cost of the first year of hosting the Flip Portfolio, (Au$40.00 value).

This is only the second Flip Portfolio to be published. The other is a Mega Flip portfolio with two hundred pages of colour photographs.

All published Flip Portfolios will be listed on the web page below:

http://www.flipportfolio.com/Published-Flips/published-flips.html

A Mega Flip Portfolio similar to the one already published will cost more than the standard Flip Portfolio. A standard Flip Portfolio supplied as a PDF file ready to be published will be up to thirty pages in length and will cost Au$140.00. You can have any size up to two hundred pages. The cost of larger portfolios supplied as ready to publish PDF's will be at the rate of Au$1.00 for each additional page.

To find out more about Flip Portfolios go to:

www.FlipPortfolios.com

Before your Flip Portfolio can be published, you will need to declare that you have the copyright, or permission from the copyright holder, for all photographs that you wish to publish in your Flip Portfolio.

Supplying a PDF file is not the only alternative for you to have your Flip Portfolio published. There are several others.

The files can be supplied as a Word document, or Libre Office or Open Office file. It can be a series of files to be combined if you so wish.

We will even accept your photo files as jpeg's and do all of the formatting for you. Yet another alternative is for us to also do your photography, or arrange to have your photography done for you. This last option will of course be dependant upon your geographic location.

There will be additional charges for any options except for supplying the complete PDF's. But, we can give you quotations for this before going ahead with the work.

Contact details and web site links are on the last page.

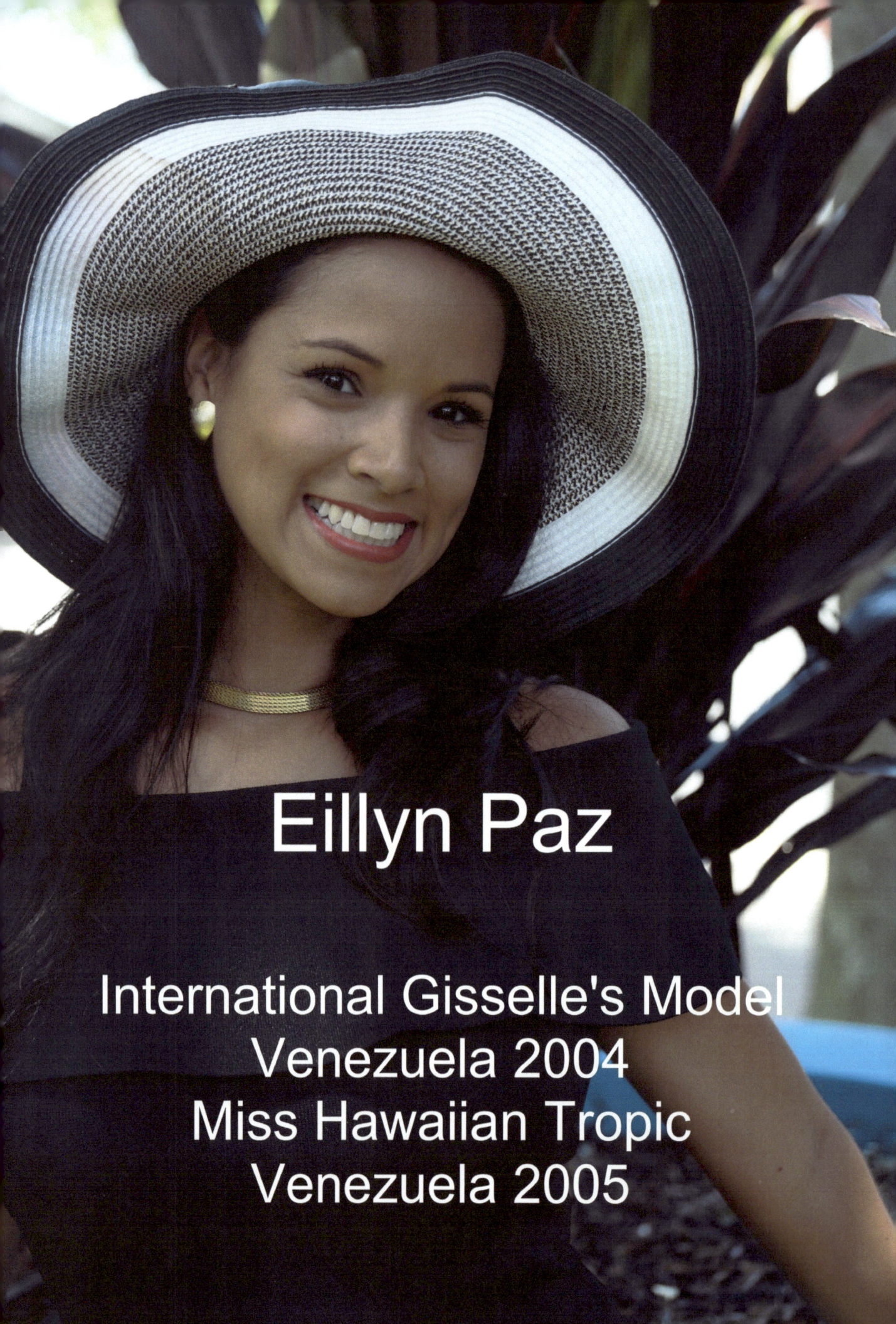

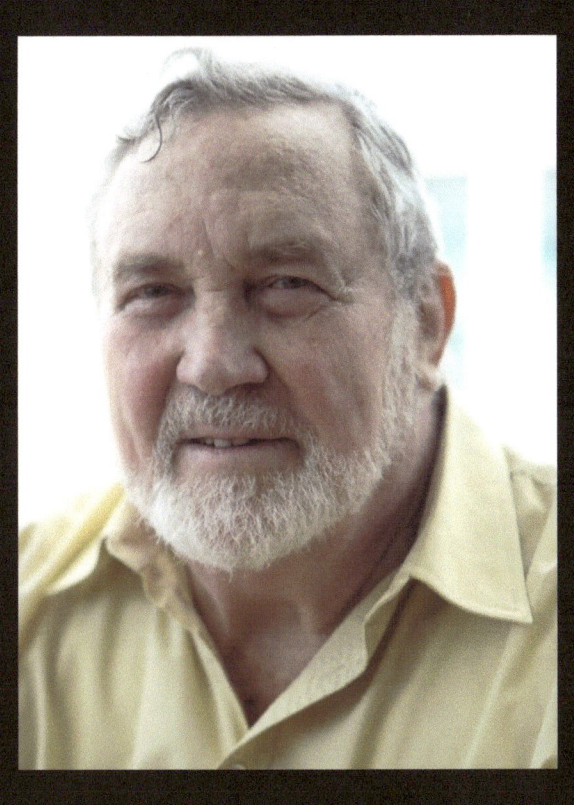

The owner of Flip Portfolios is:
Ian McKenzie

ph: +61 403 543 827
admin@aheadfoto.com

some relevant web sites

www.flipportfolio.com
www.aheadfoto.com
www.flippagemags.com
www.petographymagazine.com
www.modelsactorsperformers.com
www.southeastqueenslandliving.com
www.iansbooks.com
www.iandoesphotography.com
www.passionateaboutphotography.net
www.iandoesphotoart.com
www.petspics.biz
www.ozzi.ws

www.ingramcontent.com/pod-product-compliance
Lightning Source LLC
Chambersburg PA
CBHW040454220526
45473CB00004B/1636